A CHILD DIES

A PORTRAIT OF FAMILY GRIEF

Second Edition

◆

Joan Hagan Arnold

Penelope Buschman Gemma

The Charles Press
Publishers
Philadelphia

To Rick, Michael and Matthew
J.H.A.
To Pat, Jon, Ben and Alexandra
P.B.G.
And to the families who have shared their memories with us

Copyright ©1994 by The Charles Press, Publishers, Inc.

The Charles Press, Publishers
Post Office Box 15715
Philadelphia, Pennsylvania 19103
(215) 496-9616 - Telephone
(215) 496-9637 - Fax
mailbox@charlespresspub.com
http://www.charlespresspub.com

5 7 9 11 12 10 8 6

Library of Congress Cataloging-in-Publication Data

Arnold, Joan Hagan
A child dies: a portrait of family grief / Joan Hagan Arnold and
Penelope Buschman Gemma — 2nd ed.
p.   cm.
Includes illustrations and bibliographical references.
ISBN 0-914783-72-6
1. Bereavement — Psychological aspects. 2. Children — Death —
Psychological aspects. 3. Brothers and sisters — Death —
Psychological aspects. 4. Parent and child. 5. Family
psychotherapy. I. Gemma, Penelope Buschman. II. Title.
BF575.G7A76 1994
155.9'37'083 — dc20
94-1057
CIP

Erica Doctorow, Fine Arts Consultant
Lucinda Geist, Book Cover and Design

Printed in the United States of America

FOREWORD

If I were to recommend one book to grieving families and health professionals concerning the catastrophic experience of a child's death, it would be this one.

Joan Hagan Arnold and Penelope Buschman Gemma speak powerfully with practical advice and penetrating understanding of the suffering, loneliness and despair of the death of an infant, a younger and older child, and the crushing impact upon the bereaved family.

With compassion and sensitivity they unlock our hearts to climb through tortuous agony to valuable insights and guidance.

Yes, sadness is found within these pages. But the essential message is of the human spirit's capacity to dare to heal, recover and transform tragedy into higher levels of growth and triumphant living.

The deep truths and exquisite beauty will bring solace to many grieving hearts.

RABBI DR. EARL A. GROLLMAN
Author: *Living When A Loved One Has Died*

PREFACE

Birth and death are monumental events, the cornerstones of existence. They are moments that evoke the greatest joy and sorrow. At these times, those experiencing the beginning or ending of a life – parents, family members, friends and caregivers – either come together in cohesion, understanding, support, or awe, or they move apart in solitude, loneliness and pain. Through grieving, we learn how to continue to live in the world with our losses. How we engage in the grieving process seems to influence our potential for healthy living and relating to others.

The meaning of the death of a child to a family is the focus of this book. Children are not supposed to die. It is an experience that is unique and like none other. The death of a child is a senseless injustice. A child's death — whether expected or unexpected, regardless of age and cause — is incomprehensible. Family members ache with the pain of powerlessness and vulnerability and live with emptiness. The family is never whole again; a significant member is missing.

During the years following the death of a child, silence among survivors often ensues. To speak about a child's death is often considered unnatural, unwise, too threatening, too painful. How can families who suffer and live with emptiness gain from this sort of silence? This book is an attempt to bring to the surface what has been silenced in order to portray a child's death and the family's loss.

How can one become sensitive to the specialness of a child's death and communicate compassion and understanding to the family? Is empathy possible? There are no answers to these questions. Rather, we seek to explore the issues that these questions raise and to draw child death into the realm of critical concerns and dilemmas that need to be faced openly.

In our clinical practice, we have worked with many families after their child's death and have been touched by the extent of their pain. We have been humbled by their strength to go on and to live without their child. Families have shared with us haltingly and openly when words and expressions could only convey the fringes of their emotions and experiences. We wish to speak for the families who have chosen to share their grief with us, so that the special meaning of a child's death can be told.

We had assumed that writing this book would be less difficult than it was. In the process, we tapped into our own beings and experiences. We tried to sort out the similarities and differences between our impressions and approaches before attempting to analyze and present the data in a clear and meaningful way. We became recorders of this critical life event. The subject was painful for us to address. In the same way, you may find this presentation of child death from a personal, experiential point of view, stripped of protective jargon, difficult to read.

We have also focused on family bereavement following the death of a child member; that is, the wide range of grief reactions and behaviors that families use to express the experience of their loss. We have purposely refrained from presenting data that deals with individual and family psychopathology in response to the loss of a child, but not because these reactions are not important and do not require attention. Indeed, this topic deserves special consideration. Rather, we have sought to make visible the invisible — the vast expanse of grief after a child's death. We have focused on child death spanning the life process; families grieve when their child dies regardless of how old the child is at death. Just as the family grieves the death of an unborn child, an infant, a young child, an adolescent, so, too, does it grieve the death of the adult child.

It seemed to us that much of the clinical literature on parental bereavement was inadequate because it failed to convey the magnitude of parental grief. We turned to the artist for a more accurate portrayal. In a variety of art forms we found poignant validation of the timeless, boundless nature of the grief of parents who have lost a child to death. In his book *What Is Art?* Tolstoy wrote, "The business of art lies just in this, to make that understood and felt which in the form of argument might be incomprehensible and inaccessible. Usually, it seems to the recipient of a truly artistic impression that he knew the thing before, but had been unable to express it."

This book has been written for the many families who will benefit from sharing the experiences of others who have gone through this tragic loss. We hope that it serves as a form of support and validation for their feelings and experiences. We have also written for the relatives, friends and community of grieving families who want to gain understanding from their loved ones grief.

Finally, *A Child Dies* has been written for the many caregivers of bereaved families with the hope that the insights provided will enable them to offer meaningful support and understanding to families who have lost a child.

Joan Hagan Arnold
Penelope Buschman Gemma

CONTENTS

CHAPTER ONE

The Meaning of Loss

Each substance of a grief hath twenty shadows.

William Shakespeare
Richard II

L ife is filled with loss. It is inevitable in the experience of living. It is inescapable, yet necessary for growth. In its broadest sense, the experience of loss is a universal continuing part of the life process.

Often loss occurs without notice and may be as imperceptible or as natural as the changing of seasons, the shifting of tides and the rotation of the earth. We lose yesterday and gain today. Loss is all around us, in all life forms, and within us as cells are formed and die, in the same way that we leave childhood behind and move on to grow and change and die. Some losses carry with them deep emotional responses such as sadness, hurt, bewilderment, rage, guilt and fear. These emotions are felt regardless of how much is

---

William Dobson. Portrait group, probably of the Streatfeild family (c. 1642-3). Oil on canvas. Courtesy of the Yale Center for British Art, Paul Mellon Collection.

The Streatfeild Family, William Dobson, British, 17th century. A deceased child is not only included in this portrait of an English Puritan family, but is decidedly its subject. As the mother, tenderly affected, points to the child (draped unlike the other family members), the father casts his eyes on a death's head resting upon a cracked column. The family's hopes lie with the surviving children, the younger of whom, like infants in every age, tugs at his father's clothes for attention. *

* Reprinted from *Images of Childhood: An Illustrated Social History* by Anita Schorsch, with permission from the author and The Main Street Press, 1979.

A WOMAN OF THE MOUNTAIN
KEENS HER SON*

Grief on the death, it has blackened my heart:
It has snatched my love and left me desolate,
Without friend or companion under the roof of my house
But this sorrow in the midst of me, and I keening.

As I walked the mountain in the evening
The birds spoke to me sorrowfully,
The sweet snipe spoke and the voiceful curlew
Relating to me that my darling was dead.

I called to you and your voice I heard not,
I called again and I got no answer,
I kissed your mouth, and O God how cold it was
Ah, cold is your bed in the lonely churchyard.

O green-sodded grave in which my child is,
Little narrow grave, since you are his bed,
My blessings on you, and thousands of blessings
On the green sods that are over my treasure

Grief on the death, it cannot be denied,
It lays low, green and withered together,—
and O gentle little son, what tortures me is
That your fair body should be making clay!

Padraic Pearse (1879-1916)

* Reprinted from *The 1916 Poets*, Allen Figgis and Co. Ltd.
Publishers, Dublin.

gained in growing and evolving as a result of the loss. Loss leaves one feeling empty. Some empty spaces can never be filled, and some spaces that are filled still feel empty.

The process of life involves both gains and losses. A rhythmic pattern evolves. Time moves on and changes occur. One receives and one gives away. One wins and one loses. We look forward to the gains, and we delight in the joy of discovering what is new and different, in the freshness, specialness and uniqueness of each new experience or change within or around ourselves. Change is preferred, because we value highly the process of growing and developing. We celebrate our gains. But growing and developing also mean moving away from, detaching, letting go, giving up and losing.

Losses are grieved. Dealing with feelings of loss does not come easily. Losses are not greeted readily; indeed, they may be feared and denied. We search and long for what we have lost. Loss hurts. It is the hurt in life that we hope to soothe, hope to quiet and cover, hope to repair and recover from as quickly as possible. It is difficult to welcome and accept losses; rather, we prefer to hold on to what we have.

Loss has other meanings apart from the natural flow of life's energy and patterns. It also means being robbed, divested, denuded. To suffer loss often means to undergo deprivation, to be depleted, separated, wanting and lacking. Loss may mean to have no longer, to be gone forever. Loss can evoke feelings of horror.

Deep loss is most often experienced through death. Death can occur instantaneously, in that instant forever changing our lives. Yet nothing else remains the same. The rest of life continues. One who is living is also dying all the time. We treat life and death as if they are opposite, incompatible states of existence or opposing ends of the continuum that we call the life cycle, a beginning and an ending. They are not at war with one another but are part of each other. Living and dying, growing and losing are one process. We grieve continually. The nature and extent of our grief vary in intensity and meaning. Sometimes we are more conscious of grief and can better cope with it than at other times.

We cannot really achieve a state of resolution because loss through death is permanent and our grief continuous. The pain of loss is difficult to deal with, for the loss object will never be

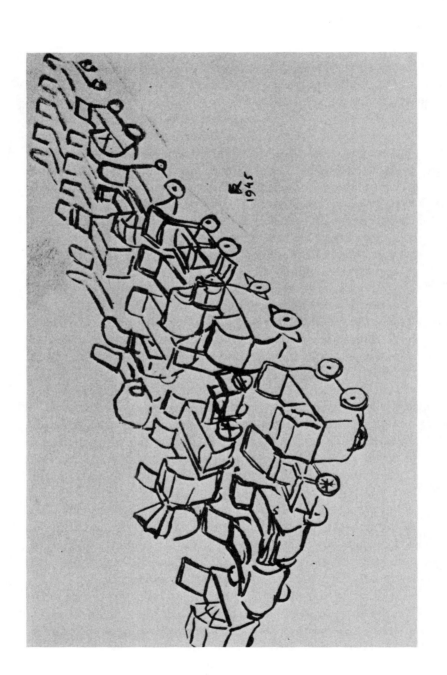

recovered. There is no way to return once one has moved on. There is no way to recapture, to relive. There is no way to grow in relationships once they are lost. What do we do about our losses? What do we do with our feelings? We bury them, live with the memory, try to forget, try to hold on in some way to what was, and idealize. In today's world there are specified times when it is all right to expose our true feelings, but generally they must remain private, stored in the depths of our experience. We move away from persons who share their losses too willingly or openly.

Losing and grieving a loved one transcends familial, societal and cultural boundaries. Although the significance of the experience may be generalized, the management of the experience may differ from one family and cultural group to another. How we recognize the loss, how we measure the importance of loss, how we ritualize expressions and behaviors are among the differences that set us apart from one another.

Loss produces change in the lives of the individual, family and society; and its impact depends on its nature and scope. Often the pain of loss comes with the need to give up that someone or something precious to us. When someone is taken from us, we do not let go willingly. There is a peculiar physical violence to loss by death, a sudden and powerful force. We do not participate in the letting go; rather, we feel as if the person we long for has been stripped, torn and severed from us and we are left feeling separated and unconnected. As John Gunther writes in *Death Be Not Proud*,

---

Francis Reisz. *Kinderwagen*. Hôpital Bichat, Paris, 1945. Ink on paper. Reproduced with permission of the artist's daughter. From *Temoignages sur Auschwitz*, edition de l'Amicale des Déportés d'Auschwitz, dessins de Francois Reisz, Paris, 1945.

Kinderwagen commemorates the death of untold numbers of children of Gypsy families imprisoned in Auschwitz and exterminated with their families in 1944. Francis Reisz recalls the loss he and other survivors felt when early one morning the Gypsy campsite was silent as the smoke from the gas chambers filled the air. Rows of baby carriages, once full of joy and life now empty, were efficiently lined up at the exit from the gas chamber building.

"What is Life? It departs covertly. Like a thief Death took him." One remains in pain and sadness with the problems of reordering one's existence, often with little recognition and support.

Though our losses may bring on profound and painful times for us, others may be unaware of how deeply hurt we are. We may feel out of step with the movement around us, but the movement does not stop for us. Nothing stands still when death occurs.

We have come to legitimize this process of dealing with sorrow by calling it grieving, mourning, or bereavement. Much attention has been devoted to this working through of loss. Attempts are made to record and analyze the behaviors of the bereaved. Commonalities in experience are searched for to develop a schema to help others study and understand the progression of this state and to delineate boundaries for normal and abnormal behavior. But grief cannot be contained; it knows no boundaries.

It defies classification and categorization. Grief is too large, too complex. Grief is everywhere and cannot be reduced or ordered. To talk about grief means accepting first that words can neither describe adequately its emotions nor convey its pervasive pain. Putting grief into words reduces its power. It is an empty effort to contain it. Grief is limitless and powerful. But we must talk to each other about our grief and acknowledge that we can never know for sure another's pain. Each person's response to loss is an expression of coping, and no one way is better than another. Each person makes meaning out of loss. We share what we can. Sharing helps to bind us by deepening our relationships and reducing the isolation that we feel.

Grieving is a process that involves coming to terms with the loss: learning to live without, learning to live with emptiness, to make meaning out of deprivation, to rejoin and carry on differently. We long for what we have lost. We search for meaning and significance in the pain and emptiness that we feel. We need to order events and circumstances so that they become comprehensible, explicable, rational and reasonable. We wish for what could have been. We wonder why, and we feel deprived and angry, empty and powerless. Regardless of our hopes and desires, of the promises and commitments that we make, a life taken cannot be returned. What is lost through death cannot be regained, reclaimed or reconnected. We must learn to cope without, to adjust to the changes, accept the emptiness, integrate, and move on.

It is difficult to feel lonely, separated and unconnected. When bereaved, one feels out of touch with the rest of the world, stigmatized, deprived and angry for being selected to suffer. One wonders why, but rarely is there rhyme or reason. It seems unfair and unjust that life deals such pain for us to bear. Those who have not had experience with death tend not to recognize or understand the pain that comes with losing a loved one. It is expected that the bereaved should grieve but grieve "appropriately"—that is, within the specifications of socially acceptable behavior. They may cry, but only so much; sulk and stare blankly, but only for so long; feel helpless and unable to participate, but only for a short time. We are expected to get up, pull ourselves together, tuck our pain and agony away, and stop the flow of tears. We are supposed to live again, to behave as though grief is over and behind us. Traffic moves, appointments are kept, and, as time passes, fewer people ask about feelings. Yet for the bereaved it is as though life has stopped within. We feel that we, too, have died. Death moves in to occupy and possess us, to join with us and be part of us.

The experience of a new loss brings back feelings associated with previous losses and previous pain. We reach into the past to childhood and feel hurts of long ago. All that has been lost throughout life is longed for anew. We wish to reclaim our losses and the tenderness and affection of relationships that are gone. We want to feel whole again. It is difficult to let go, yet letting go allows us to grow and change without the attachments that might hold us still and leave us feeling anger, frustration and guilt.

Loss connects one human being with another. The experience of loss and finding meaning in it is a process that binds the caretaker to the sufferer. In this sense, it is a human phenomenon. Loss is an equalizer.

The loss of a child is a loss like none other. A child's death is the death of innocence, the death of the most vulnerable and dependent. The death of a child signifies the loss of the future, of hopes and dreams, of new strength, and of perfection.

For parents, the agony of losing a child is unparalleled. When a child dies, a parent dies. A vital part has been severed. Parents grieve the dead child for the rest of their lives, never to be whole again. Only memories remain.

Loss leaves memories and these cannot be taken from us. As John Irving in *The World According to Garp* says, "Death eventually separates everyone from each other. It is only the vividness of memory that keeps the dead alive forever." Memories soothe and comfort us. They are ours alone in solitude and ours to share with others if we choose. They bring us recognition of what we had. They stand as an unshakable account of our past. These imprints from our past bring joy, sorrow and pain. We can shape and form our memories to give us comfort, approval and support, or remorse and guilt. Memories alter in time, perhaps becoming idealized, perhaps vague, but they still belong to us. We keep close to us memories of those whom we love and have lost.

*I shall become a dream, and through the the little opening of your eyelids I shall slip into the depths of your sleep, and when you wake up and look round startled, like a twinkling firefly I shall flit out into the darkness.... He is in the pupils of my eyes, he is in my body and in my soul.**

From *The End* by Rabindranath Tagore
Translated from the Bengali by the author

* Reprinted with permission of Macmillan Publishing Co., Inc. from *The Crescent Moon* by Rabindranath Tagore. Copyright 1913 by Macmillan Publishing Co., Inc., renewed 1941 by Rabindranath Tagore.

CHAPTER TWO

Children
and Parents:
A Family
Perspective

T o appreciate the impact of child death on that complex system that we term the *family*, we must stand back and look carefully at the whole as well as at its components and qualities. Each family system is unique, possessing characteristics that are different from all others. Families differ in their culture, history and tradition as well as in patterns of communication, work and organization. A

Edwin Romanzo Elmer (1850-1923). *Mourning Picture* (1890). Oil on canvas. Courtesy of Smith College Museum of Art, Northampton, Massachusetts. Purchased 1953.

*Edwin Romanzo Elmer's painting of 1889 achieves a complete fusion of the living with the dead. The Elmers had one adored child, Effie. They lived in a house Edwin had built before their marriage. After Effie's sudden death, her mother's grief was so extreme she could no longer bear to see children and would not remain in the empty house. Before they moved away, however, Edwin Elmer took up brush and canvas to commemorate their life together. He painted Effie, her pets and toys, his wife and himself in mourning dress, all in front of their house. Elmer's work, an end product of the posthumous mourning portrait genre, most dramatically illustrates the American wish to mitigate death's finality through art.**

* Reprinted from Phoebe Lloyd, "Posthumous Mourning Portraiture," in Martha V. Pike and Janice Gray Armstrong, A Time to Mourn: Expressions of Grief in Nineteenth Century America (Stony Brook, NY: The Museums at Stony Brook, 1980), p. 85.

family's culture, history and traditions are its links to the persons and experiences that were part of a past flow of life. They provide for the family a special flavor that comes from the blending and meshing of ethnic backgrounds, patterns of speech, values and mores as well as the true and distorted stories of how the family grew, who was born and who died, and the ways in which the family celebrated its special events and times. Culture, history and tradition are connecting points for a family and provide a means for constancy and continuity in the face of social change and upheaval.

Composition, of course, differs from family to family. One may be the traditional nuclear family including mother, father and children, or the group may include the parents, children and members of the extended family. Social changes are reflected in the increased number of single parent families with one parent assuming primary responsibility for the nurture and care of the children. If parents are separated or divorced, the second parent may share in some way the financial and emotional responsibility for child care. This role may be assumed regularly and consistently or erratically, and sometimes not at all. An adult companion of the single parent may be invested in the care of children. This companion may be a relatively stable presence over a long period or may be replaced. Extended family members, friends and child-care workers may also assume some responsibility for the children.

Assumed and assigned roles also differ from family to family. Parents traditionally provide child care and share the responsibilities. In many families there is no longer rigid adherence to traditional male-female duties and assigned tasks. More often the roles shift according to need. Many mothers have re-entered or have never left a field of employment. Fathers may provide care for the child or, if they are fully employed, may share in child care and in the other tasks of maintaining a home.

There is tremendous strength in the fabric of some families, in which bonds and loyalties are firm, conveying warmth and a sense of support to members in need. There are others whose fabric is weak and torn, so that members must extend their network outside the family to look for sources of strength.

The degree to which members of a family are connected to one another yet separate from each other is an important measure of function. There are families where the connectedness supports growth and fosters individualism necessary for the child member to separate, assume responsibility and integrate family history. There are other families who enmesh and entangle members, impeding or preventing the child's growth and ability to move on. There are still others who are splintered and broken, where members have been abandoned by the other members.

ON BEING A PARENT

Within the family system there are special relationships. The primary one between parent and child is comparable to no other relationship in its uniqueness and complexity. There is a connectedness between parent and child that has its roots in the biological and emotional bonds and attachments that precede birth. It grows as the parent begins to know and care for the child. A child is part of the self and a separate being all at once. The child is a parent's link to the future, the guarantee that life will go on. The parent's life is embodied in the child.

The relationship of parent to child is characterized by its potential for intimacy. The child who is conceived by the parents or adopted into their family is watched and listened to until even breath sounds are familiar, sleeping-waking patterns known, and needs understood. As the child grows, the parent can be an active participant in the developmental process, encouraging and fostering the child's innate ability to learn, to acquire and master new skills, and to grow. With growth is the recognition of separateness, the realization that the child, who was physiologically part of the parent, remains emotionally part of the parent but becomes in some respects a stranger, growing and unfolding.

The characterization of the parent-child relationship is the responsibility of parent to child (and conversely, in more subtle ways, the child to parent as the latter grows). The parent creates the child's life and is primarily responsible for sustaining and protecting it, shielding it from the dangers that threaten it, actual and imagined. There is also vulnerability in the relationship, the potential for grave hurt and disappointment. Parents are threatened by what might happen if they are not vigilant in protecting the child. The child might be hurt, maimed, or killed, taken unexpectedly. At the same time both power and a powerlessness exist in the relationship between parent and child. There is power to determine certain decisions and directions when the child is young, but a lack of power to protect and prevent from all harm and threats. Ambivalence characterizes the relationship as both positive and negative feelings emerge in response to the child. The parent can experience guilt when feeling anger and disapproval toward the child.

To become a parent, to grow into parenthood is a most difficult task. Becoming a parent is a process that takes place over a lifetime. It begins with the experience of being parented and the quality of that parenting. Parents may decide to make changes in the way their child is reared, but the foundations laid firmly and squarely in their own childhood are never forgotten. One must be nurtured in order to nurture. Being a parent is also an opportunity to create a different pattern and to depart from one's own past. Parenting allows a new identity and chance to make a difference.

There is a time to begin to prepare for parenting, consciously during pregnancy or while awaiting the arrival of an adopted child, a time to imagine oneself a parent, to practice, to gain skills and information, and to make room physically and emotionally for the small person who will become such a central focus in one's life. There are many ways to prepare for the arrival of a child, from the reordering of one's work and social schedules, travel and leisure plans, to the shifting of furniture and space, purchasing of items necessary for care, and calling on friends and family who have experience, wisdom and ease with children. While becoming a parent and while parenting, a parent develops certain expectations for the child, some realistic, some based on personal experiences, and some on wishes, hopes and dreams. The parent shares these expectations and actively plans for and with the child.

ON BEING A CHILD

In each of us is a child. This child is the composite of experience and memory that has been influenced by our own temperament and shaped by relationships with our families. Formed by the special needs that were met and unmet and the important developmental issues and life experiences that link us to others, the child part is always with us, interpreting and responding to the world and to those with whom we live.

We identify the child in the adult, in ourselves and in others. Conversely we see ourselves in our children—in the same eyes, nose, mouth, or temperamental bent. They symbolize the intimacy, closeness and connectedness between parent and child, and the continuation of our own existence. It is the unknown in the child, the qualities that unfold as the child develops, that surprise and excite. The parent recognizes that part of the child is unknown while at the same time intimately known.

The child grows and changes in response to the amount and level of nurturing and protection that is experienced in the family and community. The growth process is constantly in motion. The developmental potential in each child is essentially unknown. Measurements are crude at best. There is no way of predicting how far genetic, temperamental and constitutional limits can be stretched if the environmental factors that mold and influence are supportive of growth. The child may grow within the family or growth may be thwarted.

This developmental potential exists in every part of the child's being, in cognition, in emotion, in creative spirit, in socialization as well as in the physical body. As the child grows, new skills are acquired. The child shifts from a concrete, limited appreciation of the world to an expanded view allowing for thinking and reasoning more fully. The child is curious and asks questions to acquire knowledge. Even before this cognitive shift occurs, the nurtured child can move from an egocentric world view to one that includes and is affected by the thoughts and feelings of parents, siblings, important friends and others. However, the creative potential in every child is less well known. That imaginative spark can be kindled until it bursts into the flame of an idea, a symphony, a beautiful work of art, a wonderfully funny joke. In some children the potential can be recognized early. In others it becomes evident as the child grows. For some, potential is never realized.

Children embody their parents' hopes and dreams, providing a link to their past and the future. Children are unique persons, separate from their families yet connected in lasting ways.

SOCIETY'S VIEW OF THE CHILD

There is an apparent contradiction in our society about the value of the child. Although recognized as precious and in need of nurture, protection and stimulation in order to grow, legislative and societal sanctions can hinder and prevent this growth. Through its practices, our society, which claims to value children, often neglects to protect them. While the child clearly has value to the family, parents and siblings, the child's limited place in society is in question. Society is ambivalent toward its children, simultaneously giving lip service to the importance of today's children being tomorrow's responsible adults while shifting focus away from programs and funding geared to improving the lot of children and families. It is important to realize the existence of this discrepancy.

A child's contribution to society is considered minimal. Also valued little by society is the child's status and rank. However, the child is protected, nurtured and socialized by the family in preparation for future contribution to society. Thus the family is responsible for the child it values. The family is responsible for preserving and sustaining the child until he or she can take a part in adult society. When a child dies, the family is left to feel in some way it has failed in its task. Society does not recognize when a child dies that a valuable family member has died; in fact, it provides very little support for the family in grief.

There was a time when child death, although devastating, was expected. Death was commonplace and a child's death not unnatural but one of the many burdens that a family was forced to accept. Disease was rampant and children were particularly vulnerable. Families were larger, perhaps to assure parents that some children would remain if one or more died.

Those who grieved were recognized by their symbols and actions. Today the bereaved are anonymous. Funerals are recognized for their ritualistic and therapeutic value, yet when families and friends gather they disperse soon after. There is little time to grieve and little recognition given to the bereaved. Shortly after a death, one is expected to gather together the pieces of life that remain and resume routines almost as though no lapse had occurred. There is social pressure against the prolonged and public expression of personal grief. One is expected to wipe away any sign of acute grief, to reduce and cover intense emotion, and to regain control—as though to deny the very existence of one's loss.

When a child dies, this urgency to wipe away grief is more exaggerated. The social pressure toward denial of loss becomes pressure to deny pain, sorrow and loneliness and therefore finally to deny the very existence of this precious and loved child. What is it about a child's death that makes parents part of an underground of bereaved? For the most part, families who grieve for their children are alone, often isolated. The armband and mourning garb no longer exist. Who is to know which of us has lost a child? The bereaved, silently longing for their children, are all about us.

The horror of a child's death has become so frightening to us that we seek to protect ourselves, as though the germs of death could be disseminated as easily as they were in centuries past. We fear contamination, if only in an emotional sense. We do not want to be touched by the demon that takes children to their death. In these times children are not expected to die. We choose to battle with death, expecting to conquer it with our abilities and strengths. We marvel at medical knowledge and technology and expect miracles. We believe in our knowledge and machines so much that when death wins, we find it difficult to accept defeat. Defeat seems impossible, unbelievable. We exclaim, "No, it cannot be!" and refuse to accept its finality.

A child's life is precious and each child's death is a penetrating, agonizing blow. Parents may grieve forever and live with the memories they have of their child. And each memory is vivid and dear, painful and comforting. The death of a child member affects individual members and the whole family system. It may cause an alteration in family structure and in the members' roles. The strengths and values of the family may be questioned as members turn to or away from the family for support and comfort. Death of a child member becomes an important identifying piece of information about the family. It is woven into the history and the everyday operation of its members' lives. The child who has died continues to be a family member after death. Parents are forever parents of a dead child as well as of the surviving children. The dead child lives in memory. The family grieves for the child and remembers the child with little comfort and support from the society around them. The family of a child who dies lives without that child's physical presence and actual contributions but with only memories, wishes, dreams and hopes.

THE RECALL*

The night was dark when she went away,
and they slept.
The night is dark now, and I call for her
"Come back, my darling; the world is asleep;
and no one would know, if you came for
a moment while stars are gazing at stars."

She went away when the trees were in bud
and the spring was young,
Now the flowers are in high bloom and I call,
"Come back, my darling. The children gather
and scatter flowers in reckless sport.
And if you come and take one little blossom
no one will miss it."

Those that used to play are playing still,
so spendthrift is life
I listen to their chatter and call,
"Come back, my darling, for mother's heart is
full to the brim with love, and if you come
to snatch only one little kiss from her no
one will grudge it."

Rabindranath Tagore
Translated from the
Bengali by the author

* From *Collected Poems and Plays of Rabindranath Tagore*. By permission of the
Macmillan Company, New York, 1951.

CHAPTER THREE

The Process of Grieving a Child's Death

There is no relationship like that of parent and child. It is unique and special. It is incomparable in its complexities, responsibilities and vulnerabilities. The bond between parent and child is so powerful that its strength endures time, distance and strife. Despite this strength, this relationship between parent and child can be threatened. A child's life can end.

Parents live with vulnerability and dread, knowing that their child can be taken from them, that their child can die. This is an everpresent, silent fear for parents, a threat that enters their dreams and fantasies. Parents continuously battle this sense of dread and try to hide it in the deepest well of their being. As it creeps into consciousness, it paralyzes and leaves the parent impotent to prevent, alter, or forbid it. That death can occur regardless of the degree of parental caring and carefulness is a frightening reality. No one can anticipate all dangers or change the course of events which inflict hurt or cause death.

To be a parent is to be vulnerable. Parents ache with the knowledge that their greatest vulnerability lies in their inability to shield their child completely from death. Death is always possible, lurking, unforeseeable, final and irreversible.

To be a parent means having to be responsible. Central to all parenting responsibilities is the sustenance and maintenance of the child's life. Surrounding this core responsibility are loving and

---

Käthe Kollwitz. *Death Seizes a Woman* (1934). Reproduced by courtesy of The Galerie St. Etienne, New York.

MATERNITY*

One wept whose only child was dead,
New-born, ten years ago.
"Weep not; he is in bliss," they said.
She answered, "Even so,

"Ten years ago was born in pain
A child, not now forlorn.
But oh, ten years ago, in vain,
A Mother, a mother was born."

Alice Meynell

* From *The Poems of Alice Meynell*. Courtesy of The Bodley Head, London.

sharing, giving and guiding, believing and supporting. But the very essence of parenting is assuring and protecting life. A child can die in an instant—suddenly by accident, violence, suicide, illness—or after long and painful days of suffering. Death may be unforeseen or known and anticipated. Regardless of the time that it takes or the form that it chooses, parents are helpless. Death repudiates their wish to protect and rejects their plea of "not me, please not my child!"

No loss is as significant as the loss of a child to a parent. Children always remain part of their parents and connected to them. As children's lives unfold, there is the potential for the realization of the parents' hopes and dreams. The child is the future. Parents are left feeling unwhole without their child. The dead child's space remains empty. The parents' emptiness is part of their very being.

A parent's grief is for the separate person that has filled life with uncountable experiences and brought comfort, peace and love. It is also grief for the empty space within, the space that cannot be occupied by anyone or anything again. The child who occupied that space, a vital part of the self, has been torn away. The loss is physically violent and painful as the child's life is severed from the parent. The body compensates to cope with this loss. Grieving, the healing process, attempts to seal and protect the space of the child for the sake of the parent's integrity and to preserve the relationship with the child.

On the death of a child, the parent feels less than whole. The sense of self is diminished. The parent's self-esteem is shattered, for the foundation of this significant role has been shaken. The longing for the child and the feeling of emptiness may last a lifetime. A parent grieves forever when a child dies. Parents are forever parents of their dead child. Although the magnitude and intensity of grief will change with time and events, it does continue. It may even provide comfort and solace, it may bring joy in remembering the child and the love shared. Or it may reduce one to despair, to tears of loneliness and longing, and feelings of hopelessness and worthlessness. A child's death seems unnatural and unjust. When a child dies, the loss is not resolved. Rather, the parent continues to grieve, and grieving becomes a way of learning to live without the dead child and with only the memories. Death ends the child's life but it does not sever the bond between parent and child. They remain connected regardless of death. Grieving becomes a way of keeping connected. Searching and yearning for the child as the means of reuniting and reestablishing a connection continue despite the fact of death. Grieving keeps memories alive and retains a place in the family for the dead child.

The nature of grief on the death of a child cannot be described adequately. No schema can contain it; its breadth and depth defy description. Grieving is a continuous process with peaks, valleys and plateaus; it is a complex process that varies with each individual. Many have attempted to define carefully the process of grief, identifying major tasks, steps and stages, but we know little of the length of time grief takes nor the nature of its unfolding.

Parental grief is boundless, complex and everchanging. It cannot be categorized or ordered, nor can it be justly described. It is lifelong and compounded by previous losses and how they were dealt with. With time the pain of grief will lessen. One could not survive if the pain continued to be as intense as it was at the time of death. However, without warning and often synchronized with special events or remembrances of the child, the pain returns as if the death had just occurred. The valley is deep and wide, the emptiness pervasive. Grieving the death of one's child becomes a process of learning to live without the child and embarking on a journey to search for meaning where there is none and answers to unanswerable questions: Why did my child die? Why me? What made this happen to me?

The questioning is endless. Self-blame, guilt and feelings of failure can plague parents who fear that they must have been responsible in some way for the death. Self-accusations undermine all logical explanations. No reason is sufficient to explain the death of a child. There is no justice or justification in a child's death in the parent's mind.

Memories can help to soothe the pain. They can offer comfort as the dead child is remembered and as the attachment to the parent is maintained. Parental grief is not easily explained, as its expressions are intense and diverse. Parental grief may even approximate accepted descriptions of pathological grief. Healthy grief responses for parents faced with their child's death may appear

ON THE DEATH OF HIS CHILD*

O brightness of my bright eyes, how art thou? Without thee my days are dark; without me how art thou?

My house is a house of mourning in thine absence; thou hast made thine abode beneath the dust: how art thou?

The couch and pillow of thy sleep is on thorns and brambles: O thou whose cheeks and body were as jasmine, how art thou?

Faydi (d. 1595)
Translated from the Persian by E.G. Browne

* Reprinted with permission of Cambridge University Press from *A Literary History of Persia*, 1962.

extreme, bizarre and prolonged. The parent as well as the concerned observer feel the lack of guideposts to clarify natural versus disturbed grief responses.

Parents may describe a profound emptiness or feeling of deadness inside. There is a senselessness to life. Life could end and it would not matter for their reason for living is gone. The injustice of losing one's child leads some parents to challenge beliefs and values while others hold to their beliefs as a stabilizing force. Expectations of what is reasonable, good and just in life can be changed dramatically.

The death of a child assaults parents' sense of self-esteem and leaves them to question their ability to care for their surviving or subsequent children. There is seemingly no middle road. The perception is that any event or problem will inevitably result in death. The parent feels less a person, less a parent, diminished and less able to make decisions and judgments. For some parents, the child may have been the only source of pleasure and gratification in a life of deprivation and wanting. The child may have been the embodiment of the parents' wishes, hopes and dreams. Without the child, there is nothing.

Parents love to give their children what they most wanted for themselves but never had. When their child dies, there is no recipient for those special gifts. Parents continue to give their love, wishing for a response and finding none. The relationship is no longer reciprocal. Death only takes away. It forbids the continuation of sharing in each other's lives and denies growth in the relationship. The future is only what could have been, the dreams of what might have been. The memories are of yesterday so the joy of continuing to grow and share in the life of this child is denied.

Many parents are left with anger. Anger may be felt toward the dead child for leaving, and this may be difficult or impossible to acknowledge. The anger becomes woven into other relationships and unrelated situations. The parent may be angry toward the spouse, in some way blaming the partner for the child's death. Others involved in the child's world may be blamed. Anger may be directed outward toward families with children for their happiness and toward families who do not realize the treasure that they hold. Anger is also directed inward, in the form of self-blame, self-hatred and shame. This inner rage may manifest itself as depression, violence and self-destruction.

Grief is a solitary experience. Even when surrounded by other people, the parent feels alone. The normal patterns of relationships are disrupted. A strange de-synchronization pervades all of life. It is as though life moves on and the parent is left dazed and out of step, out of harmony with the pace of life and relationships. The parent is alone in grief and out of touch so that the magnitude of the loss cannot be communicated or acknowledged. There are no words to express the parent's feelings. Language is inadequate. The cries of grief cannot be heard. For some the cries of grief cannot be put into words. Parents may try to contain their feelings deep inside, fearing the enormity of their grief as a volcano threatening to erupt.

The parent continually searches for some remnant of the child. Families may choose to leave the child's room as it was, as if to preserve it so that the child's memory and place will be lasting. Parents may forbid any dismantling or putting away of the child's things for a time. The room may be a place in which to cry or to feel the presence of the child, or it may be sealed off like a museum or shrine, not entered because it is too agonizing to accept the loss. Life goes on as it was and death is rejected. Eventually the parents may be able to allow the emptiness to occupy them and grieve for the dead child.

Parents experience this loss in every part of their being. Their bodies hurt, aching with emptiness and fatigue for which there is no respite. The parents may not be able to sleep or may find in excessive sleep an escape. Nightmares and dreams of the child are common. Patterns of concentration are interrupted. Wishes for the dead child may bring the child's image, voice, touch and footsteps into the parent's thoughts as if the child were there. The expression of parental grief knows no bounds. The parent may even fear insanity.

REACTIONS TO PARENTAL GRIEF

There's a grief that can't be spoken
There's a pain goes on and on....*

Families grieving for a dead child receive inadequate recognition for the intensity and significance of their loss. There are no labels to establish the bereaved parent as someone who has experienced a significant loss. If a husband dies, the wife is called a widow. If a wife dies, the husband becomes a widower. Likewise, if a child loses the parent, the child becomes an orphan. How do we recognize the parent of a dead child?

Perhaps parents are not given recognition for the intensity of their loss because a child's death is not fully recognized as the significant loss it is. In our society, it is in living over a period of years that value is attained; the value of life is weighed in terms of the number of accomplishments or quality of achievements. The child is not felt to have contributed much in such a short life. It is assumed that a few short years of memories are grieved faster or more completely than many long years of relating. Rather, it is the nature of the relationship and the meaning of the dead child to the survivors that is significant. Or do we deny parents their anguish because of our unwillingness to confront the intensity of such a loss? We deny and push away painful expressions. The reasons may be multiple, but the outcome predictable; that is, parents are insufficiently recognized, appreciated and supported in their grief for their child.

Typically, bereaved families are shunned by others, who see their grief and look away. It may be that death itself is feared so that onlookers fear contamination. Death and tragedy may spread to them and consume their happiness. Rarely will others accept the dead child's clothing or possessions for fear that death accompanies them. Others want the bereaved parents to hide their agony because it makes them feel uncomfortable and evokes their own fear of death.

* "Empty Chairs at Empty Tables" from the musical *Les Misérables*.

Rather quickly family members learn that if they cover their feelings, they will be better received than if they show their wounds and share their feelings. As a result, a vast number of grieving parents go underground, often unconnected even to each other. It is difficult to derive acceptance and support from others who are afraid, threatened and unwilling to share pain.

Sharing in loss helps to validate the parent's experience and offer needed acceptance. But for many people, a sense of impotence and helplessness pervades, hampering their ability to reach out. Powerlessness takes over as onlookers try to convince themselves that they do not know how to help or what will help and therefore leave the bereaved parent with empty phrases or in solitude. They hope that the bereaved parents will get on with living, forget and mobilize their energies to be productive again. Grieving parents may be greeted with impatience and frustration for not recovering fast enough or for continuing to remember their dead child.

Reactions to parental and family grief are varied. More often than not, parents receive inadequate recognition and support for the devastating loss that they have experienced when their child dies.

> *...the globe tilts farther every day from the time when they lived, carrying me farther from them every day, if only I could stop its revolving....*
>
> Lynne Sharon Schwartz
> *Disturbances in the Field*

CHAPTER FOUR

Death Before Birth and During Infancy

And can it be that in a world so full and busy,
the loss of one weak creature makes a void in any
heart, so wide and deep that nothing but the width
and depth of vast eternity can fill it up!

Charles Dickens
Dombey and Son

The most beautiful and magnificent gift is life itself. A baby is exactly that, new life, the antithesis of death. This new life offers boundless possibilities for loving, caring and growing, for purity, discovery and hope. A baby is a remarkable, sensitive, competent and capable human being.

A baby is conceived out of intimacy and the parents' desire to join their love in creating a new life. This new life embodies more love than had been known. A baby also comes from a desire and decision to bring into their lives a child to have as their own, through the process of adoption.

Pregnancy or the time of awaiting an adopted child may be long and mysterious. Much time is spent waiting. With time and growth, the new life becomes more familiar. The parents develop an attachment to their child long before the child is known. The child comes from them and yet is a stranger to them, a new, separate, emerging person. The coming of the child is a welcome time, a time of greeting and getting to know someone long awaited. It is also a time when one's fears and fantasies are reduced or realized. Reality takes over as the parents meet their anticipated child.

A baby represents the hope for new life, new beginnings. With the dilemmas and disappointments of life, this creation is close to perfection and perhaps the only act of perfection achievable. A

Pablo Picasso. "Mother and Dead Child," composition study for *Guernica*, May 9, 1937. Ink on paper. Copyright ©1993 by ARS, New York/SPADEM, Paris.

baby is someone to whom love can be expressed without fear, question, or reservation. Coming from us, being part of us, a baby cannot be taken away. For those who are deprived of wealth and possessions and even dignity, a baby is all of these and something that one cannot be stripped of by circumstance or external decision.

A baby represents hope for the future, hope of a better life, hope of greater opportunities, a reaching beyond. Contained in a baby are the parents' identifications that are carried within for all times. A baby represents the potential for fulfilling dreams, a way of starting over, another chance to alter the course of a lifetime. A baby is dreams and fantasies.

A baby evokes fears and responsibilities. There is the fear that life can be snuffed out quickly, that some accident might end this dream, or that disease or catastrophe will surround life and consume it. The helplessness of the infant evokes in the parent an awareness of the awesome responsibility to protect the child and sustain the life that has been created.

A critical feature of normal development during early infancy is the experience of oneness for parent and child. The infant remains connected to the parent and continues to be dependent on the parent for the fulfillment of wishes and for nurture. The parent has become a person with a new identity, a parent of a child. The parents' physical and emotional identity is extended beyond themselves and through their infant child. Parents accept this role as a commitment. They expect to provide for their child. They will give love to sustain the child and hope that this life will be better than their own.

The complex and ever evolving relationship of parent to infant child is typified by many unknowns as each gets to know and love the other. The relationship is also characterized by ambivalence. The baby is welcomed and greeted with wonder and desire by the parents and yet they may feel the need for distance and reprieve. The parents may lose and grieve the style of living they knew before the child arrived.

New life is celebrated. The baby brings joy, embodies dreams and fantasies, and alerts the parents to the enormous responsibility that they have undertaken. Parents expect to see their children grow and mature. They hope to live long enough for grandchildren to be born and grow. Ultimately parents expect to die and leave their children behind, able to manage well with direction and purpose. This is the natural course of life events, the life cycle continuing as it should. The infant then is the hope of life's new beginning. A baby is least of all expected to die.

Each infant has a special reason for being and meaning to the parent. Each baby has a special personality and place in the family with expectations for the future. The baby may signify the culmination of a loving relationship between two people or be thought of as an accident, a form of punishment, a means to establish independence, or an object to fill an empty void. Each baby comes into a preexisting set of circumstances and relationships. The meaning that the baby carries for each member of the family will be reflected in the experience of grief and loss expressed by them. Death strikes in the midst of the complexities of these developing relationships.

Children are not always planned for and do not necessarily come at the right time. A young woman of fifteen, overweight and childlike, lived with her elderly, adoptive parents. She became pregnant by a very popular schoolmate who used hallucinatory drugs regularly. She was thrilled to have been noticed and to have been loved, but she knew little about her own body and about pregnancy. She successfully concealed her pregnancy from her parents. Terrified and unsure about what was happening to her body, she delivered quite prematurely, alone in her bedroom. The parents heard her cries and went to help her. They were overcome by what they found. The baby, born with multiple anomalies, lived for many months in a neonatal intensive care unit until he died. The grandparents and the mother visited regularly. There was no preparation for the child, no planning, and he never lived at home. But he was deeply missed and grieved.

In another instance, a young mother lived alone with her baby, who suffered from debilitating heart disease. For the many months that he lived she held him all day long, guarding his life while she cooked and cleaned and even when she used the bathroom. She was relieved by a friend to sleep a few hours or to shower. The mother did everything that she could to keep her baby alive. When her son died, the mother's grief was overwhelming, her emptiness agonizing, despite her knowledge that he would die.

A baby's life holds much meaning. Having a baby may be a way of giving love and being loved. It is a way of building self-esteem and feeling pride and accomplishment. A baby can provide a reason for living and become a bridge to the future. For some, living in poverty compounds the nature of life's dilemmas and offers few, if any, alternative solutions for coping. People living in poverty have little control, with few options. Often a baby is all that is truly their own. A baby's death becomes the ultimate deprivation. Life is stripped of all meaning, senseless, unjust and inhumane. This is particularly poignant when one considers that many infant deaths occur in families living in poverty. For some parents this assault may epitomize their powerlessness and remind them of the deprivations and dehumanizing experiences that they have already suffered. For others, this may be their first association with death.

DEATH BEFORE BIRTH

An infant that dies before birth is grieved as a wished-for child. The parents may feel completely cheated and empty, for their child was denied life and they were denied the opportunity to parent that child and to realize their dreams. Birth and the delivery of a new baby conclude the long process of anxious waiting. Fantasies are confronted and expectations are born. Birthing a baby is an act of creation and a deeply personal sense of pride swells in parents when their child is born. A baby is born into a room of joyful faces and extended arms, ready to greet and nurture. Grieving parents are denied the triumph and joy of birth and the celebration that comes from sharing their sense of accomplishment with others. Grieving parents are prevented from experiencing this time of confrontation in which wishes, dreams and worries are finally realized. When a baby dies before birth, death fills and consumes the parents. The dead child is born into a silent room. Tears flow quietly when the baby is wrapped and removed in a painful hush. Parents are left feeling an enormous void that is created when death is born.

Many unknowingly assume that when a infant lives only a short time or dies before birth through miscarriage, stillbirth, or abortion, the loss is not as great as the loss of an older child, who has lived

On the Death of
His Baby Son*

I will never be able to stop my tears.
And the day is far off when I will
Forget this cruel day.
Why could we not have died with him?
His little clothes still hang on his rack
His milk is still by his bed.
Overcome, it is as though life had left us.
We lie prostrate and insensible all day.
I am no longer young enough
To try to understand what has happened.
I was warned of it in a dream.
No medicine would have helped.
Even if it had been heaped mountain high.
The disease took its course inexorably.
It would be better for me if I took
A sword and cut open my bowels.
They are already cut to pieces with sorrow.
I realize what I am doing
And try to come to myself again,
But I am exhausted and helpless,
Carried away by excess of sorrow.

Su Tung P'o (1036-1101)
Translated from the Chinese
by Kenneth Rexroth

longer and is well known. It may be expressed that a baby is not yet fully developed as a real person. The baby may not be perceived as a productive and contributing individual. Therefore, a baby's death is often valued less by others and by society as a whole. Somehow it is falsely assumed that not enough time has passed for the child to be missed significantly. Attachments formed by the parents and family are not recognized as deep and lasting. Less recognition is given to the child's identity and meaning to the family. This may be particularly so for the baby who is born before time or delivered dead and therefore is less tangible. However, the relationship between parent and infant is powerful. A lasting attachment has been formed that endures despite the brevity of the child's life. Parents grieve deeply for their baby dead before birth and for what they will never know.

One particular mother was not given the opportunity to see or hold her stillborn child. She was also prevented from planning or being present for the burial of her child by a family that sought to protect her. This woman's fantasies about her child became nightmares. She searched and searched for some representation of her child. She needed desperately to identify and hold her baby, to make contact with her child and to feel whole again.

> I kept searching for something. I wasn't sure what it was. All of a sudden one day in the kitchen, I spontaneously got out my kitchen scales and started weighing fruits and vegetables. I realized I was trying to find something that had the identical weight that the baby did....I found myself weighing my rolling pin...and it happened to be the identical length and weight that the baby was.
>
> G.W. Davidson
> Understanding: Death of the Wished-for Child

Parents often search for ways to feel whole again when their baby dies. They yearn to feel their baby next to them. The empty uterus aches. A common reaction of others is to suggest to parents that they have another child as if it were possible somehow to replace the lost child with a new one, to wipe out their pain. This attitude also implies that it is somehow easier to replace a baby

PIETA*

Once only, with one hand,
Your mother in farewell
Touched you. I cannot tell,
I cannot understand

A thing so dark and deep,
So physical a loss:
One touch, and that was all
She had of you to keep.

* Eight lines of "Pieta" reprinted with permission from Angus and Robertson (UK) Ltd. from James McAuley's *Collected Poems*.

than an older child, who has made more of a mark on their lives by virtue of the years of living and sharing. But this infant cannot be replaced or forgotten.

Grief on the death of an infant is manifested through a wide range of normal expressions of grief. Grieving is a process of making meaning of loss and life without the baby. The baby is an important person with feelings and responses, whose personality and presence will be missed. The growing relationship and the joys received from the infant's capabilities are profound. This death is the ending of a sensitive, capable human life. Caring for that child cannot end with death, it continues on. Because the thought of death is so intolerable and permanent and the emptiness so pervasive, the only resort is to think of the baby as alive or present in some way. The parent will continue to perform the tasks of parenting. A parent may awaken to listen for the baby. Seeing the baby or hearing the baby cry are common occurrences. Some parents wonder whether the baby is warm enough in his grave on a cold day and protected from the rain on wet days. These experiences can be terrifying because the underlying fear is of insanity.

The death of an infant is too difficult to imagine. The parent wishes to return to times when life was happier and more fulfilling and the infant was totally dependent on the parents. They gave life through love and continued it through protection and nurturance. In spite of the infant's death, the parents still seek to love and protect. Their sense of worth was expressed in their ability to give life, and now they feel themselves dying, too. Continuing to care about the infant preserves their identity as worthwhile parents.

Although getting through the whole day after an infant's death is a most difficult task, nighttime is especially painful. It is quiet and uninterrupted. Thoughts are free to wander and there is a special sense of aloneness. The aloneness can be aggravated by relatives and friends who refrain from speaking about the baby.

Michelangelo. Head of the Madonna from the *Pietà*. St. Peter's Basilica, Rome. Reproduced by courtesy of Fabbrica di San Pietro and Phaidon Press Limited, London.

Unfortunately this attempt at protection intensifies the parents' loneliness, confusion and rage. Parents feel cheated and they are fearful that they will lose the memory of their baby forever. Denying the infant's being is denying their own existence.

Sleep is difficult to achieve and is interrupted by nightmares and frightful images which leave parents filled with remorse and fatigue. Sexual patterns may be altered. Partners may not share the same feelings or needs. Disagreement may cause tension between them. Some women will find themselves wanting sex more often, wanting to become pregnant to fill the emptiness. Some may be terrified of another child, fearing that every child they conceive will die. They may fear sex because of the possibility of another pregnancy and more suffering. Some may feel cheated and filled with hatred at the sight of another pregnant person or at families with thriving babies. Some will feel anger at the world for their injustice, anger with God for being selected for suffering, anger with the baby for dying and leaving. But comfort may be found while lying together and holding each other, asking no more of each other. This shared intimacy may provide needed support and acceptance.

Photographs taken of the child while alive and at the time of death become an important link. Cherishing pictures of the baby, being frightened to view them, treasuring sacred mementos of the child, and talking about the baby are ways of grieving, ways of keeping connected. To keep close to the child, the parent may pin an article of clothing such as a piece of the baby's T-shirt to an undergarment. The blanket in which the baby was wrapped at the time of death may never be washed and be saved, for it continues to hold the smell of their baby. Sometimes the baby's clothes and furniture are saved in an effort to keep the memory and presence of the dead child alive. Parents may also wish to share these loved objects of their child with relatives and friends, who often find it difficult to receive, for fear that death comes with them. Some parents leave the baby's room as it was, preserving it like a shrine, and find comfort in it. Frequent repetition of stories involving the events and circumstances of the baby's life and death become a way of reliving and keeping connected with the baby. Often the grieving family finds that they need to take the initiative and convey to others their need to talk about the baby.

During a home nursing visit some weeks after her baby's death, a mother greeted the nurse with warmth, as if she were an old friend even though they had never met. She began talking about her child, from her pregnancy through his death. Her child's room was still very much alive despite his death. Brightly colored, striped sheets decorated the crib that had a mobile above. His dresser was filled with his clothes. His certificate of birth was framed and hung on the wall. The room was intact and much like a museum, for it preserved history, the family history. The mother was unable to put anything away. Relatives and friends had completely stopped talking about the baby, denying his existence, in their attempt to help this mother cope with her loss. She could not let go of her child and refused to give in. She was going to keep her child alive in the only way that she could. The house would remain as it was when he had been alive. Further, she began to realize that if she put things away, she would be accepting his death. She had fears about her own ability to cope with her loss. She felt that she would go mad from anguish and never stop crying once she started.

Another mother described her grief this way. She said that wherever she went she saw her child, in supermarkets, on television, in the eyes of another child, and sometimes in his carriage, where he often had taken his nap. Her own body served only to remind her that she was a parent without a child while her breasts continued to fill with milk.

The day's mail with coupons for diapers and baby magazines tests the parent's strength and fortitude. The world is filled with children who remind and make the bereaved parent feel jealous and cheated. Some parents feel a need for distance and may give away the baby's clothing, furniture and other mementos, trying to wipe out reminders. Many parents will move to a different home, feeling that they cannot live in the same place that they lived with their child. It is often difficult to locate a family after their child's death.

Whether one searches for the child or searches for distance, there is no real peace. There are no reasons for the death of their child. A baby's death will always seem senseless. A baby is a part of the parents, less a separate person and more an extension of them. A baby is pure, perfect, amazing and dependent, new life with new hope. A baby is part of the parents' self that can reach beyond their dreams and wishes, giving them a feeling of satisfaction and a sense of creativity and gratification that cannot be found in any other relationship. Each memory is important, each memory is seared to the parents' very core. The dead child will always be a baby, a dream of sweetness and perfection.

ON THE DEATH OF A
NEWBORN CHILD*

The flowers in bud on the trees
Are pure like this dead child.
The East wind will not let them last.
It will blow them into blossom.
And at last into the earth.
It is the same with this beautiful life
Which was so dear to me.
While his mother is weeping tears of blood,
Her breasts are still filling with milk.

Mei Yao Ch'en (1002-1060)

CHAPTER FIVE

Death of a Young Child

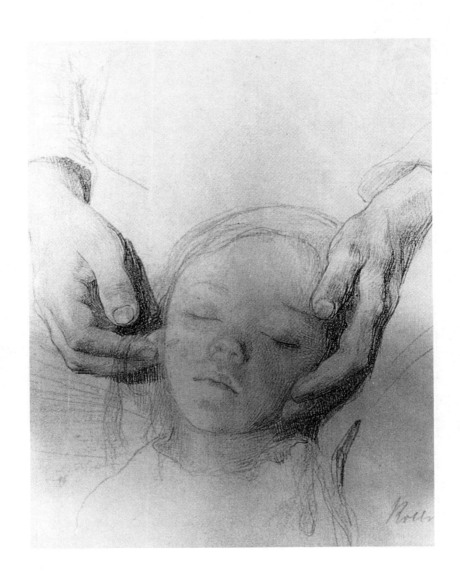

The death of a young child is a special and devastating loss for a family. This child, while connected to the parents through dependency and vulnerability but no longer a baby, has become a more separate individual in the family. Temperamental patterns apparent during infancy have been translated into day-to-day working and playing and relating. With growth, there is recognition of the abilities and talents as well as limitations. The young person is discovered, becoming fuller and more recognizable. The qualities that resemble or reflect parental and sibling ways have become visible, while at the same time, the unique characteristics of the personality unfold in a mysterious way. The young child grows and changes from day to day, makes a mark on the world, and in return is influenced by it. The magic that we term *development* occurs within the child in the context of the family and reflects what is allowed and fostered by them.

The child through play and work moves into wider areas of exposure outside the family. The young child plays with friends, attends school, begins to negotiate with other adults and children. Responses are elicited from the parents, siblings, other family members and friends that range from positive to negative. The child is rewarded and punished, praised and corrected.

The growth of the young child is fostered by the need to separate from the parents in an effort to develop individuality, to become a

---

Käthe Kollwitz. *Child's Head in a Mother's Hands*. Reproduced by kind permission of the Staatliche Kunstsammlungen Dresden.

A Mother To Her Dead Child*

...The earth: she is too old for your little body,
Too old for the small tenderness, the kissings
In the soft tendrils of your hair. The earth is so old
She can only think of darkness and sleep, forgetting
That children are restless like the small spring shadows.
But the huge pangs of winter and the pain
Of the spring's birth, the endless centuries of ruin
Will not lay bare your trusting smile, your tress,
Or lay your heart bare to my heart again
In your small earthly dress....

My little child who preferred the bright apple to gold,
And who lies with the shining world on his innocent eyes,
Though night-long I feel your tears, bright as the rose
In its sorrowful leaves, on my lips, and feel your hands
Touching my cheek, and wondering, "Are those your tears?"
O grief, that your heart should know the tears that seem
    empty years
And the worlds that are falling!

                                                Edith Sitwell

separate self. Parents struggle with this process of separation and individuation, fearing for the safety and well being of their child apart from them. The dilemmas of parenting are paradoxical at this stage. Parents wish to foster growth yet fear harm and the random occurrence of death. There is a growing awareness that haunts parents that despite all effort and love, there is no guaranteed safety for their children. Magnifying this fear is the reality that accidental deaths do occur all too frequently. Moments of paralyzing fear invade awareness as thoughts of death take over. Fostering the child's growth requires that parents push aside these fearful thoughts which heighten their vulnerability and impair their judgment. The developmental issues which typify this age compound parental grief.

When a young child dies, left behind are large empty spaces in the family structure. Because the young child is fully connected to the family and occupies a special space in that system, the loss will be most keenly felt there. The child's unique personality is missed and so, too, are contributions in the form of the special tasks, responsibilities and roles. In addition parents may mourn their expectations of who the young child might have been or might have become. The parents' wishes, hopes and dreams about their child are never realized. The child's potential is hinted at but never fully developed. They long for the love given so freely, the sparkling face filled with joy, the endless questions about how things work and why they happen, the pure reactions and responses, the thrill and excitement of new experiences. Yearned for, too, are the tears that flowed freely but were transformed into smiles by the parents' touch, hugs and words. Parents yearn for a return of the treasured moments, the happy times as well as the aggravations. Parents pine for another opportunity to touch, see and feel their child. They may regret their harsh responses, the unfair expectations and the angry, negative feelings that were expressed.

Parents remember the child at the age the child died. Rituals are important as the family seeks to retain a connection to the dead child. One family shared the fact that they continued to set a place at the table for their six-year-child who had died. For this family not to do so seemed to deny the child's existence. This same family hung and filled their dead child's Christmas stocking alongside

When Thy Mother Dear[*]

When your Dear Mother
Steps in through the door
And I lift my head
To meet her glance
Not on her face
At first does fall my gaze
But to that place
Nearer to the threshold
There, where your dear, little face
Would be
When you, bright with joy
Would come in with her
As before, my little daughter

When your Dear Mother
Steps in through the door
In shimmering candlelight
It always seems that you are with her
Stealing into the room behind her
As you used to.
Oh you, joyful glow of your
Father's chamber—
Alas, too soon, too quickly
snuffed out.

> Friedrich Ruckert
> Translated from the German by
> Doris Vollinger Cappadona

---

[*] Friedrich Ruckert wrote the words for the Kindertotenlieder in 1834 after losing his two youngest children in a scarlet fever epidemic. "When Thy Mother Dear" is the third song from the Kindertotenlieder, composed by Gustav Mahler.

Gustav Mahler. "When Thy Mother Dear" from Kindertotenlieder. Used by kind permission of European American Music Distributors Corporation, sole U.S. and Canadian agent for Universal Edition.

those of the surviving sisters. Each one in the family contributed a gift that would have been appreciated by the now dead child. The gifts given over years were always chosen for him at the age he was when he died.

Photographs of the dead child may occupy a central position in the family's home. Clothing and possessions and special collections that are accumulated by most children, representing their movement from one season or one size to the next and from one interest or skill to another, serve as visible and concrete reminders of the child's mark on his widening world. What to do with those possessions becomes a problem for many parents after the child dies. Should they be saved or given away? One mother asked that her seven surviving children select the special possessions that reminded them of their brother. She put all these away in a memory box and suggested that the children rummage through the box and recall how the dead child enjoyed the various collections and toys. Her house rule was that this rummaging must not be done alone.

Memories of the child's contributions and favorite activities with other family members are cherished. One father remembered that the house in which his child had died had become a source of comfort to him, for when his seven-year-old son was alive they had once repaired shingles together. When he was especially lonely for his son, the father would look at the nails driven by the child and would remember the time shared. This memory gave him comfort.

The child known beyond the family is mourned by the circle of friends, classmates and community. The school-age child who has been involved in group activities, scouts, church groups and clubs leaves empty spaces in all of those groups. School friends and teachers have a very different collection of memories that reflect the many dimensions of the young child's life including competitiveness, rivalry, mischief and humor that characterized their interactions. One ten-year-old boy commented after the service commemorating the life and sudden death of his school buddy, "I liked him a lot, he was my friend. I'm going to miss him but he wasn't as good as they said."

Parents may find comfort in the statements of sadness and loss expressed by others who had known their child as if the child's value has been confirmed and the magnitude of the loss better

understood. One family from a closely knit inner-city neighbor-hood derived comfort from the fact that on the day of their eleven-year-old's funeral service, the streets were lined with chil-dren from the school. All were dressed in white and all carried flowers. They participated in the service, surrounding the grief-stricken parents and surviving brother. The family appreciated this touching display of recognition and support through shared grief.

Adults and children whose lives had been touched by the child who died may wish to commemorate the death in some way. Dedicating a yearbook, planting a tree, hanging a photograph, stopping activity for a moment of thoughtful reflection may help to mark the life and death of a young child.

When the young child dies, the loss is deeply felt and grieved by the family and by the circle of important friends and acquaint-ances touched by the child's life. Memories of the young child are the special possession of not only the parents but also relatives, teachers and friends.

Child's sarcophagus, depicting the Holy Bath. Roman, late 1st century A.D. Reproduced with the kind permission of Giuseppe Di Giovanni.

[Here] is depicted the scene of the whole family consisting of seven people who have gathered for the holy bath. The bath represents the respect that the child has for the Gods of the Underworld by showing himself in his dignity in order to make friends. The child who is completely naked is very nice to see. His figure is perfect. He is going to get the holy bath and he looks like he is ready to enjoy the liquid over him. The ball on the column-shaped altar symbolizes the dedication to the Gods of the child's toy thus representing the deep value of memory moved to the holy field. This was a common habit of both Greek and Roman young people. As a matter of fact, when they became adolescent, they used to offer the Gods all their toys.

* Reprinted from Giuseppe Di Giovanni, *Agrigento: The Valley of the Temples*, The National Archeological Museum, p. 121, with the permission of the author.

Overleaf: A small child's grave. Photograph copyright ©1979 by Joan Harrison.

CHAPTER SIX

Death of
an Older
Child

Adolescence is a stressful time for many young individuals and for the family systems to which they remain connected. It is a time full of unknowns and potential dangers. The safe, nurturing and somewhat predictable environment that many families have worked to create for their children is jeopardized as the adolescent moves from that setting into one that is made risky by actual and potential dangers and by the attitudes of the adolescent.

In adolescence, the child will have developed relationships and connections with friends, organizations and institutions apart from the family. Many of the struggles throughout adolescence concern the young person's effort to separate from the family and establish an identity that is unique. This developing part of the person may be strange and quite unknown to the family. As values and modes of living change and shift away from those of the family, the adolescent clearly becomes different, less recognizable. An unwillingness or inability to articulate the changes that may or may not be fully understood further removes the adolescent from the communication patterns that are characteristic of the family. The changes within the adolescent, the pull to move away from the family, and the closing down of communication may contribute to tension and confusion in the family.

The Holmes Children Stone. East Glastonbury, Connecticut (1795). Red sandstone, 48 x 45 in. From *Graven Images: New England Stone Carving and its Symbols, 1650-1815,* by Allan I. Ludwig (Middletown, CT: Wesleyan University Press). Reprinted with permission of Allan I. Ludwig.

FALL 1968*

*He's dead; and the pain is immense.
Your heart goes numb in the knowledge
that he is no more.*

*You daren't ask why he, of all people,
had to die—for you know
there is no answer.*

*And in your shock,
You notice the world doesn't stop
turning
even though he is gone.*

Glen Mitchell Gittelson
(April 27, 1956—May 25, 1971)
A Sugared Bitter Tart

* Glen wrote this poem at the age of twelve, three years before his death.

Parental roles and patterns of nurturing and caring also begin to shift and change as the adolescent grows. Anger may characterize the changing relationship between the parent and adolescent. Some parents may grieve the loss of the child during adolescence, hoping to reconnect in young adulthood. Parents feel less sure and competent with their adolescent. Questioning their own competency, parents fear for their child as the adolescent begins to grapple with the risks, unknowns, problems and experiences that await during this developmental age. Have they as parents prepared their child well enough to remain safe? Does the adolescent possess sufficient skills, wisdom and judgment to deal with and make critical decisions? In a potentially dangerous period of life where accidental injuries and suicide are the leading causes of death, parental concerns are more than justified. The emerging adolescent with changing moods and ways may not be able to impart reassurance that the parents most desperately need.

When an adolescent child dies, grief is compounded by the changing ties to the family and the parents' loss of control and influence on their child. Parents may be angry with their adolescent for having made decisions that might have contributed to the death. There may be guilt on the part of parents for feelings and exchanges preceding the death. Other parents may idealize their adolescent, selectively remembering qualities and characteristics as a way to shield themselves from accusation and blame.

Families of adolescents who die may feel less responsibility for the actual cause of death if they have allowed their adolescent child some part in decision making. However, that they allowed this more active participation then may be questioned. Were they not protective enough? Might they have prevented the death had they exercised more parental control over the child and circumstances? Indeed, part of the family's role in growing with the adolescent child is allowing more responsibility for actions, choices, successes and failures. Without this gradually increasing freedom to separate, the adolescent cannot develop the autonomy that contributes to wholeness as a human being.

Parents are often left to struggle with their own guilt and enormous sense of responsibility while they find comfort in their ability to let go. One family sanctioned the decision of their only son, a 17-year-old college freshman, to hitchhike home for a holiday time. The boy was killed on the road by an erratic driver. His heartbroken parents struggled with the fact that they had supported his decision to hitchhike home. They felt entirely responsible for his death until they recalled, with the assistance of their clergy, that they had vehemently opposed his decision. However, respecting his wishes, they had not attempted to change his mind. There was some small relief in sharing that enormous burden.

The adolescent's skills and talents and special interests are reflected in the possessions that are left behind. In many homes, in every room there are visible reminders of the adolescent whose belongings filled so much space. There are items of clothing, pieces of sports equipment, books, pictures and other belongings that marked the adolescent's presence. In the wake are left the scores of memories of the adolescent as an infant, a young child, a child of middle years. Photographs, trophies, toys and projects remain as poignant reminders of so many years of life. They both haunt and comfort the remaining family members.

The adolescent develops ties and connections to others outside the family. The grief of others can be comforting to surviving members, as the valuing of their grown child by others affirms the magnitude and importance of the loss to the family. One mother commented that she had no idea that her 13-year-old son, who recently and unexpectedly died, was so sensitive to other people. To her he appeared self-centered and absorbed in his own interests and activities while at home. The mother learned through class-mates and friends that her son actively sought ways to be available to others. She felt proud and comforted by this information about her son.

Parents are left with the sense of unfairness, the bitter disap-pointment that they have been deprived of knowing their child as an adult, as that person separate from themselves yet a part of them and their link to the future. Some parents believe that just as they have been deprived of knowing and watching this young person's growth to adulthood, the world is poorer for their child's absence.

Parental grief is always tinged with the bitterness of deprivation. Having invested so much in the life of an adolescent, to have their child taken from them is devastating. Parents are helpless, impotent to intervene, and angry. Death can take the adolescent expectedly or unexpectedly and sometimes violently, aborting the natural process of separation and individuation that is healthy and characteristic for this period.

A Word From Frances *

Frances Gunther

Death always brings one suddenly face to face with life. Nothing, not even the birth of one's child, brings one so close to life as his death.

Johnny lay dying of a brain tumor for fifteen months. He was in his seventeenth year. I never kissed him good night without wondering whether I should see him alive in the morning. I greeted him each morning as though he were newly born to me, a re-gift of God. Each day he lived was a blessed day of grace.

The impending death of one's child raises many questions in one's mind and heart and soul. It raises all the infinite questions, each answer ending in another question. What is the meaning of life? What are the relations between things: life and death? the individual and the family? the family and society? marriage and divorce? the individual and the state? medicine and research? science and politics and religion? man, men and God?

All these questions came up in one way or another, and Johnny and I talked about them, in one way or another, as he was dying for fifteen months. He wasn't just dying, of course. He was living and dying and being reborn all at the same time each day. How we loved each day. "It's been another wonderful day, Mother!" he'd say, as I knelt to kiss him good night.

There are many complex and erudite answers to all these questions, which men have thought about for many thousands of years, and about which they have written many thousands of books.

Yet at the end of them all, when one has put away all the books, and all the words, when one is alone with oneself, when one is alone with God, what is left in one's heart? Just this:

I wish we had loved Johnny more.

* Excerpts from *Death Be Not Proud* by John Gunther. Copyright ©1949 by John Gunther. Reprinted by permission of HarperCollins Publishers.

Since Johnny's death, we have received many letters from many kind friends from all parts of the world, each expressing his condolence in his own way. But through most of them has run a single theme: sympathy with us in facing a mysterious stroke of God's will that seemed inexplicable, unjustifiable and yet, being God's will, must also be part of some great plan beyond our mortal ken, perhaps sparing him or us greater pain or loss.

Actually, in the experience of losing one's child in death, I have found that other factors were involved.

I did not for one thing feel that God had personally singled out either him or us for any special act, either of animosity or generosity. In a way I did not feel that God was personally involved at all. I have all my life had a spontaneous, instinctive sense of the reality of God, in faith, beyond ordinary belief. I have always prayed to God and talked things over with Him, in church and out of church, when perplexed, or very sad, or also very happy. During Johnny's long illness, I prayed continually to God, naturally. God was always there. He sat beside us during the doctors' consultations, as we waited the long vigils outside the operating room as we rejoiced in the miracle of a brief recovery, as we agonized when hope ebbed away, and the doctors confessed there was no longer anything they could do. They were helpless, and we were helpless, and in His way, God, standing by us in our hour of need, God in His infinite wisdom and mercy and loving kindness, God in all His omnipotence, was helpless, too.

Life is a myriad series of mutations, chemical, physical, spiritual. The same infinitely intricate, yet profoundly simple, law of life that produced Johnny—his rare and precious soul, his sweetness, his gaiety, his gallantry, his courage: for it was only after his death, from his brief simple diaries, written as directly as he wrote out his beloved chemical experiments, that we learned he had known all along how grave was his illness, and that even as we had gaily pretended with him that all was well and he was completely recovering, he was pretending with us, and bearing our burden with the spirit, the élan, of a singing soldier or a laughing saint—that law of life which out of infinite mutation had produced Johnny, that law still mutating, destroyed him. God Himself, no less than us, is part of that law. Johnny was an extraordinarily lovable and alive human being. There seemed to be no evil, only an illuminating good, in him. Everybody who knew him, his friends and teachers at Lincoln, Riverdale and Deerfield, our neighbors in the country at Madison, felt the warmth of his goodness and its great vitality in him. Yet a single cell, mutating experimentally, killed him. But the law of mutations, in its various forms, is the law of the universe. It is impersonal, inevitable. Grief cannot be concerned with it. At least, mine could not.

My grief, I find, is not desolation or rebellion at universal law or deity. I find grief to be much simpler and sadder. Contemplating the Eternal Deity and His Universal Laws leaves me grave but dry-eyed. But a sunny fast wind along the Sound, good sailing weather, a new light boat, will shake me to tears: how Johnny would have loved this boat, this wind, this sunny day!

All the things he loved tear at my heart because he is no longer here on earth to enjoy them. All the things he loved! An open fire with a broiling steak, a pancake tossed in the air, fresh nectarines, black-red cherries—the science columns in the papers and magazines, the fascinating new technical developments—the Berkshire music festival coming in over the air, as we lay in the moonlight on our wide open beach, listening—how he loved all these! For like many children of our contemporary renaissance, he was many-sided, with many loves. Chemistry and math were his particular passion, but as a younger child at school, he had painted gay spirited pictures of sailing boats and circuses, had sculpted some lovable figures, two bears dancing, a cellist playing and had played some musical instruments himself, piano, violin and his beloved recorder. He collected stamps, of course, and also rocks; he really loved and knew his rocks, classified them, also cut and polished them in his workshop, and dug lovely bits of garnet from the Connecticut hillsides.

But the thing closest to his heart was his Chem Lab which he cherished passionately. It grew and expanded in town and country. He wanted to try experiments that had not been done before. He liked to consider abstract principles of the sciences, searched intuitively for unifying theories.

He had many worthy ambitions which he did not live long enough to achieve. But he did achieve one: graduation with his class at Deerfield. Despite the long illness that kept him out of school a year and a half, he insisted on being tutored in the hospital and at home, taking his class exams and the college board exams for Harvard, and then returning to Deerfield for commencement week. The boys cheered him as he walked down the aisle to receive his diploma, his head bandaged but held high, his young face pale, his dark blue eyes shining with the joy of achievement. A fortnight later, he died.

What is the grief that tears me now?

No fear of death or any hereafter. During our last summer at Madison, I would write in my diary when I couldn't sleep. "Look Death in the face. To look Death in the face, and not be afraid. To be friendly to Death as to Life. Death as a part of Life, like Birth. Not the final part. I have no sense of finality about Death. Only the final scene in a single act of a play that goes on forever. Look Death in the face: it's a friendly face, a kindly face, sad, reluctant, knowing it is not welcome but having to play its part when its cue is called, perhaps trying to say, 'Come, it won't be too bad, don't be afraid, I understand how you feel, but come—there may be other miracles!' No fear of Death, no fight against Death, no enmity toward Death, friendship with Death as with Life. That is—Death for myself, but not for Johnny, God, not yet. He's too young to miss all the other parts of Life, all the other lovely living parts of life. All the wonderful, miraculous things to do, to feel, to see, to hear, to touch, to smell, to taste, to experience, to enjoy. What a joy Life is. Why does no one talk of the joy of Life? shout, sing, write of the joy of Life? Looking for books to read with Johnny, and all of them, sad, bitter, full of fear, hate, death, destruction, damnation, or at best resignation. No great books of enjoyment, no sense of great utter simple delight pleasure fun sport joy of Life."

All the things Johnny enjoyed at home and at school, with his friends, with me. All the simple things, the eating, drinking, sleeping, waking up. We cooked, we experimented with variations on pancakes, stews, steaks. We gardened, we fished, we sailed. We danced, sang, played. We repaired things, electric wires, garden tools, chopped wood, made fires. We equipped the Chem Lab Workshop, in the made-over old boathouse, with wonderful gadgets and tried out experiments, both simple and fantastic.

All the books we read. All the lovely old children's books and boys' books and then the older ones. We read Shaw aloud—how G.B.S. would have enjoyed hearing the delighted laughter of the boys reading parts in *Man and Superman* in the kitchen while I washed up the supper dishes—and Plato's *Republic* in Richard's *Basic English*, and Russell, and St. Exupéry. On Sundays, we would have church at home: we'd sit outdoors on the beach and read from The Bible of the World, the Old Testament and the New, the Prophets and Jesus, also Buddha, Confucious, and Mahomet. Also Spinoza, Einstein, Whitehead, Jeans, Schroedinger and Maugham.

We talked about everything, sense and nonsense. We talked about the news and history, especially American History and its many varied strains; about the roots of his own great double heritage, German and Hebrew; about empires past and present, India's nonviolent fight for freedom, and about reconciliation between Arabs and Jews in Palestine. We talked about Freud and the Oedipus complex, and behavior patterns in people and societies, getting down to local brass tacks. And we also played nonsense games, stunts and card tricks.

We sailed, and got becalmed, and got tossed out to sea, and had to be rescued. And we planned sailing trips.

All the things we planned! College, and work, and love and marriage, and a good life in a good society.

We always discussed things a little ahead. In a way I was experimenting with Johnny as he dreamed of doing with his elements, as artists do with their natural materials. I was trying to create of him a newer kind of human being: an aware person, without fear and with love: a sound individual, adequate to life anywhere on earth and loving life everywhere and always. We would talk about all this as our experiment together.

He did his part in making our experiment a success. Missing him now, I am haunted by my own shortcomings, how often I failed him. I think every parent must have a sense of failure, even of sin, merely in remaining alive after the death of a child. One feels that it is not right to live when one's child has died, that one should somehow have found the way to give one's life to save his life. Failing there, one's failures during his too brief life seem all the harder to bear and forgive. How often I wish I had not sent him away to school when he was still so young that he wanted to remain at home in his own room, with his own things and his own parents. How I wish we had maintained the marriage that created the home he loved so much. How I wish we had been able before he died to fulfill his last heart's desires: the talk with Professor Einstein, the visit to Harvard Yard, the dance with his friend Mary.

These desires seem so simple. How wonderful they would have been to him. All the wonderful things in life are so simple that one is not aware of their wonder until they are beyond touch. Never have I felt the wonder and beauty and joy of life so keenly as now in my grief that Johnny is not here to enjoy them.

Today, when I see parents impatient or tired or bored with their children, I wish I could say to them, But they are alive, think of the wonder of that! They may be a care and a burden, but think, they are alive! You can touch them—what a miracle! You don't have to hold back sudden tears when you see just a headline about the Yale-Harvard game because you know your boy will never see the Yale-Harvard game, never see the house in Paris he was born in, never bring home his girl, and you will not hand down your jewels to his bride and will have no grandchildren to play with and spoil. Your sons and daughters are alive. Think of that—not dead but alive! Exult and sing.

All parents who have lost a child will feel what I mean. Others, luckily, cannot. But I hope they will embrace them with a little added rapture and a keener awareness of joy.

I wish we had loved Johnny more when he was alive. Of course we loved Johnny very much. Johnny knew that. Everybody knew it. Loving Johnny more. What does it mean? What can it mean now?

Parents all over the earth who lost sons in the war have felt this kind of question and sought an answer. To me, it means loving life more, being more aware of life, of one's fellow human beings, of the earth.

It means obliterating, in a curious but real way, the ideas of evil and hate and the enemy, and transmuting them, with the alchemy of suffering, into ideas of clarity and charity.

It means caring more and more about other people, at home and abroad, all over the earth. It means caring more about God.

I hope we can love Johnny more and more till we, too, die, and leave behind us, as he did, the love of love, the love of life.

THE ADULT CHILD

Just as the family grieves the infant, the young child and the adolescent, so do they grieve the death of an adult child of any age. The parents grieve the loss of their adult child, who is at the same time part of themselves and yet a separate person who has contributed to their lives over the years. For elderly parents who no doubt have known other losses, being predeceased by their child is intolerable and unnatural and produces a special sense of injustice and guilt. The natural order of the elderly dying and the young living is reversed. Many parents would willingly exchange their own lives for the life of their child. To have lived beyond their child seems intolerable.

How connected and involved that adult child was to the family of origin determines the grief responses of parents and surviving siblings. In their process of grieving, parents of the adult child may attempt to search out clues and reasons for the death, looking back as far as memory will allow. This process is longer and more difficult because of all the number of years that their child had lived. Distortions appear in the form of rationalization and idealization; there may be gaps in memory. Were there problems that parents had missed? In retrospect, were they to blame for something they did not see or do?

For the parent who has become dependent on the adult child for emotional support, financial assistance and everyday care, that child's untimely death produces hardship, deprivation and disruption. For parents in this situation, grief may be tinged with anger and disappointment. To have been left to fend for themselves, assisted only by friends or agencies, after a period of dependency on adult offspring is a bitter and difficult abandonment indeed. Now who will take care of them? Who will understand them as well as their own child did? Will they be responsible for the care, nurture and support of grandchildren? Sorting out the questions and problems complicates parental grief.

Parents may blame their adult child for the untimely death. If the adult child was married, they may blame the surviving spouse. Thus anger for the death may be displaced onto the surviving spouse or grandchildren, causing a rift between them. If the rift is great, changes in the availability of grandchildren to grandparents may result in another loss. The spouse and grandchildren may relocate to a distant area so that the normal visiting patterns are changed and contact with grandparents severed, compounding the latters' loss.

Parents of an adult child who has died receive little recognition and sympathy, while the spouse and children are the recipients of condolences and comfort. Cards, messages of support, phone calls are for the most part directed to the widows, widowers and surviving children while parents receive little that recognizes their enduring relationship and profound grief. Grief on the death of one's child is not bound by age or circumstance.

And you watch with serenity through the winters of your grief

Kahlil Gibran

Käthe Kollwitz. *The Parents* (1923). Woodcut. Courtesy of The Galerie St. Etienne, New York.

CHAPTER SEVEN

Living Without

Ah woe is me! Winter is come and gone. But grief returns with the revolving year.

Percy Bysshe Shelley
Adonais

Grieving is a process families engage in to cope with loss and death and to learn to live without. When a child dies, the parents learn to live without the child, while always living with the knowledge and sensation of being "parents of a child who has died." As survivors, parents are left to deal with their loss by living with pain and emptiness, aloneness and anger, and ultimately by investing their energies in relationships with others, establishing new ties with the world. In the process of grieving for their child, parents search for ways to fill their emptiness. They search for meaning and justice where there are none. After their child's death parents may wonder if it is truly possible to live. If there were only something to give or sacrifice for the return of their child's life, how willingly they would do that. Parents may think about their own death, perhaps as the only means of rejoining their child. Physically the parents live, yet death seems to occupy them. It is as though the exterior relates and responds, even happily, yet tears are shed within. The shattered survivor may move slowly, floating, drifting, apart from the outside world. Parents do not "get over" such a death. Living is learning to survive without their child. The grieving process is long—life long.

Anne Morrow Lindbergh, in *Hour of Gold, Hour of Lead*, writes: "Contrary to the general assumption, the first days of grief are not the worst. The immediate reaction is usually shock and numbing disbelief. One has undergone an amputation." Grieving is a lifelong process of learning to manage and negotiate life without a vital part of oneself that cannot be replaced. The wound may heal in some fashion, but the scar and emptiness remain. Parents change. Their relationship to one another and the family constellation and interactions are altered by the child's death. But their love and attachment to their child do not die and are not limited by time.

In the years that follow their child's death, parents will grieve for what was and what will never be. They will grieve for their emptiness. A child's death cannot be so easily accepted. How can parents give up their child to a grave?

Parents ask "Why?" but there is no answer to justify a child's death, no acceptable reason why a child should die. Parents ask, "Why me? Why did my child die? What is wrong with me? What did I do?" They must also contend with the questions that others ask them. Members of the extended family, neighbors, police, funeral directors, doctors and medical examiners seem to ask, "What did you do or neglect to do?" Blame takes over and answers some of these questions, for no real explanation satisfies.

Blame takes on other dimensions with family survivors of suicide who are left with special pain borne of unanswered questions. "Why did my child die?" becomes "Why did my child wish to die? Why did I not know? What could I have done to prevent the death?" Family members are left with guilt, sadness and rage. The cause and special circumstances of each child's death present painful questions and bewildering dilemmas which contribute to endless searching for blame by the parent. Inevitably, the search leads to the self. The parents may identify actions or omissions that they wish could be undone or altered. The parent is left to feel responsible and deprived of the opportunity to anticipate or respond differently.

Parents continue to care for their child despite death and learn to find comfort in memories. Memories keep the dead alive as they preserve and protect the lost loved one. Through memory the dead child remains a member of the family. Photographs and portraits along with clothing and small treasures are concrete memories. They are real and can be touched and held. Memories can be shared with others through stories and recollections of special days and events or words. The child can also be remembered in silence and solitude. A mother whose young daughter died many years ago commemorates her birthday each year by placing bright ribbons on the grave, a poignant reminder of the hair ribbons loved and worn by her child. The dead child is always part of the parent's memory and never forgotten.

When a child dies there is little to hold onto for solace. If the

RISPETTI:
ON THE DEATH OF A CHILD *

I thought I heard a knock on the door.
And I jumped up as if you were here again,
Speaking to me, as you so often did,
In a coaxing tone: "Daddy, may I come in?"

When at eventide I walked along the steep seashore
I felt your small hand quite warm in mine.

And where the tide had rolled up stones,
I said aloud: "Look out that you don't fall!"

Paul Heyse
Translated from the German
by E.H. Mueller

---

* Reprinted from *Poetry for Pleasure, The Hallmark Book of Poetry* by permission
of Hallmark Cards, Inc.

child's life had been filled with pain and suffering from illness or if the death was sudden or violent, parents will suffer in their knowledge of the anguish of the child's dying and death. If sweet and endearing memories are recalled vividly, they support and serve to help healing and learning to live without.

After a child has died, other children may be born or adopted into the family, but subsequent children can never replace the dead child. Joy will be felt for each new life and sadness will continue for the dead child. The wish for another child may be hampered by difficulty in conceiving compounded by illness or discord in the parents' relationship. Some relationships may not be able to grow beyond the death of the child. Separation and divorce may occur. The void between the parents deepens, leaving them far apart and unable to help each other or their relationship. For some parents a bond of intimacy and survivorship connects them. While bereaved parents fill their lives in many areas, the empty space left by the child who has died is never filled. The empty space is forever.

When a child dies, parents learn to live without their child, yet knowing and feeling that their child is always with them, always a part of them.

CHAPTER EIGHT

Siblings
and Other
Survivors

The significance of a sibling's death to the remaining child or children in a family is not fully understood. These survivors and subsequent children express in their behavior and in words the deeply felt impact of their grief.

The short-term effects include horror, distress and sadness. There is concern that what has happened to a brother or sister might in some way befall them. There is guilt that their destructive wishes, nasty thoughts or words might have possessed a power strong enough to kill their sibling. A peculiar sense of relief is felt by the surviving child in having parents home and physically present. Yet there is resentment at the parents' sadness and preoccupation with thoughts of the dead child. The surviving child feels emotionally abandoned in the face of parental grief. Intense and painful feelings of loss pervade their relationship. The pain of

---

Frederick Stiles Agate. *Mother Lamenting Over Her Dead Child* (1827). Oil on canvas. Courtesy of the National Academy of Design, New York.

Agate's Mother Lamenting Over Her Child depicts a young mother in sorrowful resignation and a despairing child mourning an infant in the sleep of death. The theme of the deceased child—popular in the nineteenth century—is underscored by an hourglass in the background, a symbol of the transience of earthly life.*

* From *All Walks of Life: Paintings of the Figures from the National Academy of Design* (New York, 1979), p. 18.

losing a loved brother or sister is profound and parental presence may not be sustaining.

Surviving siblings may respond by emulating the behaviors and mannerisms of the dead child. As an immediate response, it is protective and may elicit the praise and comfort of understanding adults and win a special place for the child in the family. Over the long period of time, it may be burdensome, impede growth and influence the development of the surviving child.

Children whose siblings die of difficult and painful diseases often develop a hypochondriacal response, imitating the physical neediness of the ill child and unconsciously substituting their own concerns for those of the parent who is emotionally distant and preoccupied. These children may express untoward fear of bodily injury or illness as a statement of their own heightened vulnerability.

Parents suffer a devastating and shattering blow to their own self-esteem and their sense of themselves as good parents. They feel that they have failed in their primary task to protect and sustain their children. The confusion and internal questioning that result affect the quality of their responses to their surviving children. Initially, at the time of death and for the acute period of mourning, parents may be quite unresponsive to remaining children, unavailable and detached, caught up in their own web of grief. The usual family exchanges about play, school and everyday matters become unimportant. The children feel parental ambivalence, the tentativeness of replies, and the suspension of sure judgment. They experience distance and confusion. Some remaining children question their value to their parents, considering the devastation that they have witnessed in their parents' response to their sibling's death and wonder why their love is not enough to fill their parents' emptiness.

The sharing of secrets, humorous happenings and observations is avoided by parents whose energies are needed for recovery and healing or who may feel that to share joy would be a betrayal of their dead child. The presence of healthy children is both welcome and unwelcome. The healthy child is the bittersweet reminder of the lost health or vitality of the child who is dead.

There is a paucity of guidance for parents in the very difficult decisions that they must make for their own children when one child dies. At best, there is controversy about the value of siblings participating in funeral and burial rituals. Little is offered to assist families in their decision making. Usually discussion involves analysis of the issue in relation to developmental abilities of particular periods of childhood. Key to all analyses of this issue is the importance of the support that these children need from their parents throughout the funeral rituals. An indication of the family's ability to sustain and support can be seen in a child's willingness to attend the funeral. The child's wishes must be listened to carefully at all times.

Some participation in the family's rituals of mourning serves to include the remaining children in a process that allows them and the parents to begin to live without the dead child and to strengthen their relationships as survivors who must continue to live together. To be excluded from the critical events following the death widens the gap between grieving parents and surviving children. These early decisions and the degree to which the grief is shared set the stage for how the loss will be dealt with in the weeks, months and years ahead. Exclusion itself is a statement of parental detachment and isolation. The children left out can think only of their presence as being unimportant, providing no comfort. They are demeaned. Their own sadness and distress go unrecognized.

Some parents may arrange with their clergy or significant support person to meet with them and their children before the traditional funeral service for prayer, quiet discussion and a time of shared sadness. The family shares this special time together, allowing the children to question, cry, perhaps to touch the coffin or flowers and see the body if they wish.

Careful description and explanation geared to the child's understanding of what will be seen and heard as well as the opportunity to review impressions and perceptions afterward are important for children of all ages. This principle also applies to the explanation of the cause and circumstances of the death. If parents are entangled in their own grief so that they are unable to provide this closeness and comfort, a family friend or relative who knew both the dead child and the living, as well as the family's religious or ideological beliefs and feelings, may be in a position to assist the surviving children or help by encouraging the parents to share their grief. In this way, strength is gained from the love among the family members.

The long-term effects are not as easy to identify and measure, for they last a lifetime. When questioned, adults remember vividly a sibling's death and their feelings with such clarity as if the death occurred yesterday. Emotions and powerful memories lie buried close to the surface and can be uncovered with surprising ease or be caused to erupt with unexpected distress.

Because the death of a child member becomes part of the history of the family, a surviving child confronts the sibling's death in many ways over time. These confrontations occur whether or not the sibling's death has preceded the birth of the surviving child. Siblings struggle with this part of their family history. They may commemorate the dead child in words and pictures on special days and events, or they may find these reminders too difficult to bear.

Communication patterns in the family determine the way in which the surviving members are able to live with the sad and joyful memories of their dead child and with their combined and separate grief. If parents speak of the dead child, if they include photographs in family clusters, they clearly give permission for the surviving siblings to remember, to ask questions and to express the thoughts and wishes that linger. One family maintained a row of photographs arranged in chronological order in the family room. These were taken of the eight children at the time of birth. Adjacent to those were the most recent photographs. Striking in that lineup of cheery, healthy faces was the last photograph taken of the dead child. The siblings born after that death argued among themselves whether they should include him as one of the eight or count only the seven living children.

One mother maintained a "cry box" containing all of the special possessions of the dead child from his kindergarten art productions to his infamous sneakers remembered by the family for their worn down, odoriferous state. The surviving children were invited to look at that box and tell or listen to stories about the contents and the child to whom they had belonged. Endless hours were spent with these pictures and possessions. The dead child still occupied a significant place within the family. Loss in the family system has many meanings. Each sibling lives with the death of a brother or sister and the accumulation of memories allowed by the family.

Each child in a family has a special meaning and place. Families will recall the child's meaning with humor and sadness and with the myriad of intense emotions that continue for one who is dead. Usually in human interchange there is a mutual and continuous interaction allowing for change and growth. These times of reminiscing about the dead child's legacy remain static and limited.

There is a range of reactions to surviving children over time. These are dependent in part on the pattern and nature of the parents' grieving process, that is, how parents as individuals and as a couple deal with this loss. One father described his reluctance to spend time with his surviving son, seemingly frightened of the possibility of deepening this relationship and then losing this son.

Some parents describe themselves as being more cautious than ever in protecting their remaining children. Activities and experiences formerly encouraged are forbidden for fear of injury. Children are kept from areas where contamination or hurt might occur. Threats may be exaggerated and distorted by the parents as they make day-to-day judgments about the safety of their surviving children.

Following the death of children, parents may consider conceiving another child immediately or adopting a child to fill the empty place that exists in the family. One father commented that should his seriously ill son die, he would adopt a boy of the same age and coloring. Indeed he would name him for his dead child and expect of him similar attributes. Other families listening to this father responded in horror but then acknowledged their understanding of his wish to provide an exact substitute for his dying son.

In a more subtle substitution process, some parents will endow their surviving children with the qualities and attributes of the dead child and will have the same expectations of the living children as they had of the one now dead. That this child cannot live up to those expectations or may exceed them is a constant source of disappointment to parents, whose primary need is to protect themselves from the pain of their grief.

Many families find in their remaining children comfort and solace and reason to go on. In an effort to confirm their capabilities as parents to their remaining children, there may be perceptible changes in their availability and care. One father left his position as an executive officer in a company and preferred to work in a less demanding position, desiring more time and energy for his family after his young son died. This father stated that his own perception of his living child changed and he treasured the time spent with her.

Surviving children sorely miss their dead sibling. Longing for the child's presence and companionship will continue over a lifetime. The remaining children struggle with issues of responsibility and guilt for their imagined or actual participation in the death of their sibling. The normal and universal feelings of rivalry become painfully accentuated when a sister or brother is sick over some time, requiring parental attention and concern. What of the angry thoughts and wishes provoked by the sick child in a moment of teasing or rage? What of the hostile acts that may in fact have contributed to a sibling's death?

There may be an enormous burden of guilt carried by the child whose action or whose inability to protect contributed to a sibling's death. For children whose guilt is great by virtue of their own fantasies or real actions, there is a pressing need for careful discussion and listening. This work, which may include the parents, often must be done with the aid of a therapist who can respond from a more neutral base than family members. Whatever the circumstances, the guilt will not dissipate unassisted. These feelings need to be worked through carefully and sensitively.

Remaining children may confound and anger parents in their ability to maintain academic performance, to enjoy peers and activities, to contribute to the family, and to continue to grow despite having lost a sibling. Indeed some children demonstrate a perceptible amount of growth in maturity. A family may denounce these responses as being egocentric, proving that the remaining sibling is unfeeling, insincere, or callous.

It is important to realize that children grieve differently than adults. A child can continue with play and work without the encumbrance of constant, unrelenting grief. For the surviving child or children the grieving process seems to be dealt with little by little rather than as the continuous process that the adult undergoes. In children, reworking grief can occur sporadically and spontaneously when memories of the dead brother or sister are touched. The nature of childhood bereavement is reflected in a combination of factors including the developmental level of the child, behavioral boundaries set by the family, and the child's own special style of relating and dealing with the world.

Grandparents, extended family members and friends grieve deeply for the child who has died and for the loss of their special relationship with that child. For grandparents to live after their grandchild has died seems to them unjust and out of the natural order of events. Many grandparents would gladly die in their grandchild's place. For them, the death of their grandchild means the ending of a relationship and the loss of a link to future generations. Their lives through the life of their grandchild will not continue. They grieve, too, for their sons and daughters who are diminished by their grief. Grandparents feel helpless, unable to comfort their children or soothe the devastating pain.

Other survivors such as friends, teachers, coaches and neighbors grieve for the dead child, for the relationship which has ended and for the loss of the child's presence and participation.

Overleaf: The Gravestone of Ampharete, holding her grandchild. Reproduced with permission from D.C. Kurtz and J. Boardman, *Greek Burial Customs* (London: Thames & Hudson, Ltd., 1971), p. 262.

Epitaph: I hold here this dear child of my daughter. When in life, we both beheld with our eyes the rays of the sun. I held her thus on my lap; and now, both dead, I hold her still.

CHAPTER NINE

Caring for Grieving Families

Wᵉ as outsiders only touch the fringes of family grief. We try to deepen our understanding so that we can be as helpful as possible in our approach as caregivers, but we are all beginners in this process. There are no guidelines, absolute answers or protocols on which to rely, no remedies or cures. Rather, we learn through involvement with grieving families. Our learning is continuous and new. The more we learn from families, the more we are awed by the intensity of grief and humbled by the lessons of the bereaved.

The death of a child presents the most severe crisis and the most significant loss for a family. This is true regardless of the age of the child, the circumstances of the death—whether sudden or expected—or the cause of the death. *When* a child dies is not indicative of the intensity of the grief response. It is no more or less painful if a child dies at three months, three years, thirty years, or sixty years of age. It is the very fact that a *child* has died that makes it profoundly different from other deaths.

If days and months or even years pass as a child is dying, the family may have the opportunity to share and prepare for the death, often with anticipatory grief. When the child does die, parents continue to grieve throughout their lives. No reason can justify the death of a child. Whether death is caused by an accident, a chronic disease, a sudden and rapid illness, suicide, or an unexplained syndrome or condition, child death is unjustifiable and incompre-

---

Hannah Höch. *Der Unfall* (1936). Collage. Reproduced with permission from Marianne Carlberg-Hoch, private collection.

95

hensible, an unnecessary ending of a life. Each family is left to deal with the circumstances and the cause of the death as only they can, as best they can. Their whys will never be answered.

The dead child is mourned forever. A parent may in some way learn to live without the child and to live with emptiness and memories of what the child was and could have been. But these families are never whole again. Nothing said or done can restore them to wholeness. Caregivers can assist families in sorting out, understanding, expressing feelings and supporting the members as they learn to live without their dead child and with each other in a productive and meaningful way.

To do this, we as caregivers must begin by looking within ourselves to examine our thoughts and feelings about a child's death and the bereaved family. Often we prematurely judge a grieving family and we question the quality of parenting. We ask ourselves if the family acted appropriately and quickly enough, we wonder what went wrong, what they did or did not do. Unfortunately these judgmental questions and doubts are communicated both directly and indirectly.

As caregivers we need to prepare ourselves to help by examining any preconceived ideas and judgments we may have. Their influence may be subtle or overt and pervasive. This self-examination is particularly important because the very essence of our interactions with families is that we ourselves are therapeutic. We as caregivers can never know enough about grief. The more we comprehend, the more we realize that we can never completely know and understand the pain and reactions of another. People touch us and we touch them in the process of sharing the pain of their loss. Yet as much as we share, we cannot truly know their pain. We gain strength from each other, from within ourselves, and by sharing even if we only know the periphery or the surface of the meaning of another's loss. There are no words to describe the pain of losing a child.

Anger is part of grief and yet it often takes the caregiver by surprise. It can frighten and distance the helper especially if the anger is taken personally and interpreted as rejection. For the family, dealing with anger becomes a vehicle that assists them to cope with their grief more effectively. Expressing anger may be a way of asking for help. As caregivers we can offer ourselves, our skilled ears to listen carefully, and our sensitivity and concern as we reach out to the bereaved. We should be there to listen, to help families find their strength and options, to promote an atmosphere of acceptance and appreciation of the meaning of their loss, and to provide an environment to facilitate the expression of grief among family members.

When do we take the time to discuss our needs, our feelings, our reactions to situations, to understand our strengths and our limitations? Working with families in grief is a very special experience. We get close to people during the worst tragedy in their lives. We treat wounds that never completely heal, wounds that cause excruciating pain. Working with families in grief means expressing our humanity, trying to empathize. As we share ourselves we also share in their tragedy. We enter another's space dominated by grief. We come close to facing death. We cannot help but be reminded of the frailty of life. We hear the clock tick, recognize the need to value each day, and try to keep close to the people whom we love, ever mindful of the care and effort needed to maintain these relationships. How easy it is to be involved in the mundane and to get caught in a web of unnecessary complexities and trivia. We are reminded of our losses, the death of people whom we have loved deeply. We are reminded as well of the unresolved relationships, the words never spoken, the inner peace that might have been, the sadness and longing, and the emptiness. We remember the conflicts, our own anger and resentment never dealt with adequately.

Perhaps we too have suffered the death of a child, a child for whom we grieve all the days of our lives. The pain of that loss may collide with the feelings that others may share with us. We bring into a caring relationship our personal histories of loss and longing for those in our lives who have died. We bring our own pain, and we are reminded of our own vulnerability. We recognize that grieving is an attempt to keep connected, to keep alive our loving and caring, and to continue our relationships in some way with those we have lost to death. We face our own fears and fantasies and know that the sadness within us will surface when we care for people in grief. We realize that death can come to us and to someone whom we love dearly in the unforeseeable future. We dread the loss of connection resulting from death.

In working with the bereaved we must come with our own

- hurts and losses,
- feelings about loss by death,
- desire to care for others,
- ability to reach out and involve ourselves, and
- inability when overpowered by the horror of a child's death and our own sadness.

One of the authors recalls a situation from her own personal experience as the coordinator of a counseling program on infant death:

Our office was located in the morgue and we were to provide on-site counseling for families who came to identify their dead infants. One of our responsibilities was to accompany the family to view their dead child. This escorting of families was a daily function. Each time I took a parent to the viewing room, I felt uncomfortable. I wanted the viewing to be as brief as possible. I focused on the difficulties that I felt parents must be having with the experience. Once while alone with a baby boy, rearranging the blanket that covered his body, I realized what was troubling me. I was afraid of his dead body, afraid to touch death—to come too close to death. After this experience, my conflict about viewing a dead child was relieved; I was more comfortable within myself and consequently I was able to be of more help to families. I was more concerned with their experience, and less concerned with protecting myself. After this experience, I was able to stay with families and listen to them speak about or to their dead child. I could simply stand in silence as they stared at or touched their infant.

This account portrays the necessity of being able to recognize personal fears as limitations when working with bereaved families. Our feelings and fears will surface whether or not we choose to deal with them. In fact, caregivers in the process of self-exploration need to analyze their motives for working with bereaved families. Issues from our past may guide or provide direction for each of us in the professional decisions that we make. While much in our past remains unexplained or appears disconnected as we work and apply our energies in the service of the bereaved, this analysis of our own life and losses is essential and basic to the process of caring. This analysis promotes objectivity, so important in a therapeutic relationship. In this we are truly caring for ourselves and developing the ability to care for another. We are therefore responsible and accountable for exploring our personal beliefs about death, loss, bereavement; about children, families and parenting; about children dying; and about our need to help to others.

As caring persons we want to help; we want to heal hurts and eliminate pain. We want to correct, to restore, to make whole again, to alter somehow the course of events that led to this end. In child death, we cannot accomplish these tasks, and we need to accept this reality. We can act through understanding, believing in the strengths of people to survive and live on, to rebuild their sense of self-esteem as parents and lovers, and by helping to restore meaning and significance in relationships as well as to create new ones.

Recommending solutions often comes easily to caregivers. We offer answers to the questions as we perceive them, solutions that make sense to us. Rather, we need to look through the eyes and feel through the senses of the family, to listen, to believe in their ability to choose and act for themselves. This approach is therapeutic in itself. Empathy is not possible in this instance, for in no way can we feel the intensity of the loss or know what it is to live through time after the death of another's child. In truth, the caregiver cannot experience the pain nor take the pain away. For the caregiver there is this tug-of-war in bereavement work. There is the desire to extend oneself and share in the pain of another and also to pull back because the pain is so big and consuming and frightening. Child death affects us all.

The therapeutic process begins by acknowledging that the death of a child is undoubtedly the ultimate tragedy; children are not supposed to die. The process of helping is an interactional process, people reaching out to each other. For the caregiver, this assumes the need for openness and a willingness to become involved. No one emerges ready to do this work. It is always difficult to begin, but we all must start somewhere. There is little balance in this work. It involves being exposed to a great deal of hurt, powerlessness, rage and emptiness. It means voluntarily putting ourselves in a hurting place. When a family calls six months or one year or ten years after a child's death, one expects it to be a call for help. It may be a difficult anniversary, a particularly agonizing time of emptiness and longing.

Being able to extend oneself in this interactional process of helping requires the ability to share and yet to remain separate. That separateness allows the caregiver to give care to another in a selfless way so that the needs of the bereaved are primary. The bereaved can be served by a caregiver who is unencumbered by personal emotional baggage.

To work in this capacity for a period of time, we must take into account our own needs. It helps to provide a regular time to listen to fellow caregivers and share feelings, to aid in each other's need to refuel. We must take the initiative to care for ourselves so that we can feel good about ourselves and our work. It is a unique agency or institution that has a support network for care providers built into the practice setting. It is also important for us to build collaborative relationships with colleagues so that they are available to relieve us when we feel overwhelmed. We need to allow ourselves to request help. A person cannot keep fresh and sensitive all the time. We need solitude and time in the form of holidays and vacations to rekindle our energies and deal with our feelings. Most of all, we need balance and perspective to help us know that children are born to grow and flourish and not always to die.

No one is unaffected by loss or exempt from feelings of grief. Sharing feelings, building collaborative networks, taking time away are essential life supports for the caregiver of the bereaved. Without these supports, distancing oneself, becoming detached, disengaged, impersonal, even unavailable are ways of trying to protect oneself from hurt. We do not choose whether or not we should grieve. We do grieve. Without taking care of ourselves or without breaks or balance in our work we may begin to experience a sense of being dissipated. We may begin to see ourselves as failures, develop negative feelings about ourselves, and experience conflict in both personal and professional relationships. We may begin to seek distance from the bereaved at the same time feeling anger and harboring guilt for this response.

These feelings find expression in family and professional relationships. Some of the warning signs of being depleted include experiencing chronic exhaustion, feeling upset, having difficulty eating or sleeping or having frequent nightmares, developing psychosomatic symptoms (headaches, backaches, weakness), feeling physically and emotionally exhausted, unhappy, trapped, worthless, rejected and pessimistic.

The emotionally depleted caregiver may begin to avoid contact with others, leave work early and arrive late. There is also the potential for the opposite to occur. The caregiver may lose a personal sense of self and move in with the family. The boundaries that serve to separate effectively one person from another to maintain individual identity begin to blur. The caregiver can get lost and not be able to navigate the morass of sadness, thereby relinquishing the ability to guide and anticipate in this relationship, which has lost its therapeutic quality. Further, we may encourage families to become reliant or dependent on us. Dependency in relationships without limits of time and space is not therapeutic.

The caregiver therefore must enter a helping relationship with a healthy sense of respect for the bereaved as separate persons capable of independent decisions and self-care. For the caregiver is present only for a time, not permanently. It is necessary to understand the risks and difficulties involved in caregiving because of the potential for further complications. A caregiver carrying unresolved emotional baggage or unable to maintain an objective perspective will only hinder a bereaved family's efforts to work through grief. Caring in a therapeutic relationship lies in the following:

- To try to be empathic in order to comprehend the magnitude of the family's loss on the death of their child.
- To be accepting and unafraid, not rejecting and limiting.
- To listen and to speak of child death, recognizing it for all that it is—an unparalleled human tragedy. We need to recognize the families' loss and ensure that they will be respected and admired for their ability to deal with the vastness of their loss. It is

important to legitimize their loss by talking openly about the dead child. To continue the silence is somehow to deny the child's very existence and to deny the parents their relationship with this special person who once lived, was a significant part of their lives, and has a place within them as long as they live.

- To attempt to resolve our own fears about death, our sense of intruding into an area of people's lives that we construe as private, intimate and personal. Grief can be shared. We need to be hopeful, recognizing their feelings of hopelessness and knowing that families can survive.
- To believe in the families' strengths and abilities to cope, to take charge of their shattered lives again, to make decisions and to rebuild self-esteem.
- To foster and maximize these strengths and existing networks of support. We should encourage families to rely on their own judgment, make the most of the supportive ties and connections that they possess and to seek new avenues of support.
- To serve as a facilitator for effective communication among family members by listening, clarifying, promoting and encouraging interchange.Through this approach we support families as they learn to live with their pain and live without their child.

Just as families search for meaning, so do caregivers. We can find meaning through the sharing of our humanity, by building connections between people and by openly facing our own feelings about child death. The foundation for working with grieving families is our caring and open attitude and our desire to listen, understand, appreciate and accept feelings and experiences. No one person is better prepared to deal with grieving families than another. Grief and loss are not the focus of any one discipline. In truth, each of us has something unique to offer. We offer ourselves. There are no answers and no explanations adequate to justify the injustice of losing a child. But the act of caring, the sharing of one's humanity, will make the difference.

CHAPTER TEN

For Caregivers Working with Grieving Families

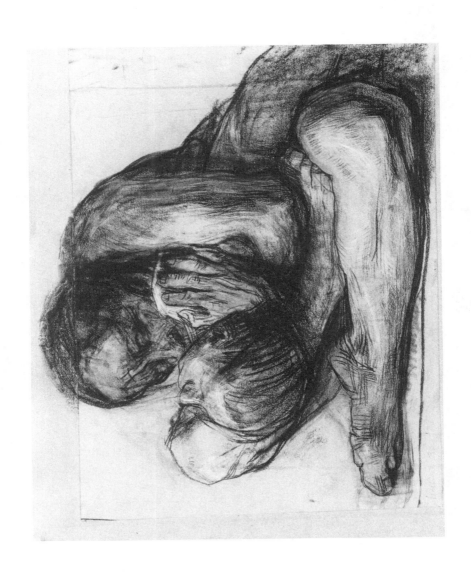

Beginning to work with a family involves internalizing the belief that a child's death has a profound impact on the family and that recognition, acceptance and validation of their experience are means of providing needed support for the anguished family. The caregiver enters a space of pain filled with sadness, emptiness, desperation, confusion and rage.

It is difficult to begin to help; who would willingly be subjected to this pain? It is no wonder that those in grief are so often asked to forget their lost loved one and go on with life. The bereaved are asked to put away their pain because it is intolerable to the outsider who may feel drained, emptied and threatened by vulnerability. In this close relationship with death through another's loss, the caregiver may also be reminded of the precious nature of life itself, to feel its wonder and to value loved ones.

Being available to another in grief means lending oneself to another. Nothing can be asked of the bereaved family. Having no expectations, the caregiver does not carry preconceived thoughts or images of how one should look or behave when a child dies. Grief is not uniform. Rather, it is a statement of an individual's coping, and there is a wide range of normal coping behaviors.

As a helper, the caregiver is oriented toward caring and curing, making better or easier, and alleviating another's suffering. Yet in grief work the caregiver can make no promise of alleviation or relief

---

Käthe Kollwitz. *Woman with Dead Child* (1903). Private collection, U.S.A. Courtesy of the National Gallery of Art.

of pain. Rather, the focus of the interaction is to assist family members in living with this pain, living with their loss. The caregiver serves as a facilitator for the expressions of grief. Working with bereaved families means accepting that the family is free to share what they choose while the caregiver's responsibility is to work with what is given. The surfaces of the experience can be shared, but the depths of grief cannot.

If we begin with concern for the family, the family will provide the direction for our interactions. Families can guide the caregiver in offering support appropriately; they can be asked what kind of help is needed. Their statement of needs may differ from those identified by the caregiver.

Families are able to make decisions in their own time and own way. Nevertheless, it is essential for the caregiver to reach out. Bereaved family members are not likely to call for assistance or for validation of their experience. Their feelings of pain may be so intense that the line between sanity and madness becomes indistinguishable. They may feel that they are losing their minds, yet asking for support may require more energy than the emotionally depleted parents have. Decision making will be especially difficult. Reaching out to families is necessary in their state of grief because they are less likely to ask for help. Home visits are particularly useful as the family is able to maintain control and the caregiver is a guest. But the family may not choose to return to the site where their child died, even if support is needed, because this journey is too painful. Outreach is required here because a common response in dealing with the death of one's child is to move. The family members may be unable to remain in their home confronted by so many reminders of the dead child. Often families stay with relatives or friends or drift aimlessly when they are unable to return home.

No one is really expert in the field of grief work. Little research has been conducted to identify the most effective strategies for work with bereaved families. We are all learning. Listening to the families themselves, who are the best teachers, will enable the caregiver to learn about the true nature of grief when a child dies. Interacting with bereaved families means engaging in a mutually defined relationship, becoming involved, giving and receiving. We convey our concern by giving ourselves and accepting pain.

Through the process of talking about the death of one's child, feelings are recognized and legitimized, and support is gained. The caregiver can then feel restored by experiencing the reviving strength of the survivors.

The caregiver should accept the family and their responses without question. Just as families are diverse in their individual styles, methods of operating, values, rules and patterns, so are grief responses unique. The caregiver should accept all grief reactions— anger, frustration, defeat, depression, guilt. The family may openly welcome the caregiver to share in their grief or close off attempts at establishing a relationship. Parents may be filled with guilt and spend years in anguish because they feel that if they had been better parents to their child, more loving, or more protecting, their child would be alive. Listening for blame requires an astute ear. Blame is always inner-directed though it may be displaced on others. Parents may blame the caregiver as well as themselves for not having the resources to have secured the best health care for their child.

Caregivers may become scapegoats for parental rage even if they never knew or cared for the child, simply because they represent the health care system that could not prevent the child from dying. It is difficult not be offended but be open and accepting when rage is directed personally. It helps to recognize the horrifying power-lessness, loss of control and painful yearning that lie beneath this surface expression. Behind the outbursts of anger are tears of helplessness that have not been given opportunity to emerge. Anger may be the only expression possible for the grieving parent.

The caregiver can assist the family members through acceptance and recognition of the intensity of their feelings and significance of their loss and assist them in identifying and clarifying their strengths. Offering solutions to identified problems does not assist the family to mobilize the needed strength to survive and grow together. By listening, the caregiver can help the family members speak to each other and identify alternatives for themselves. This approach encourages communication within the family, fosters understanding through sharing, and reduces blame.

Listening is an expression of concern. The caregiver communicates a sense of presence with the family by leaning forward, establishing eye contact, reacting to the pain expressed, perhaps touching, and conveying through acceptance a trusting attitude. Listening means accepting what is said, the themes of guilt and blame, the problems. The family may be stricken with problems aside from the child's death that can be paramount. If these problems are not attended to and remedied, grieving for the dead child can be delayed or halted.

The caregiver supports the parents by communicating a belief in their ability to parent effectively by admiring their strengths and love in caring for their children and through recognition of their love for the dead child. Communicating with the bereaved family involves

- listening,
- accepting,
- believing,
- clarifying,
- validating,
- trusting.

The caregiver seeks to work with the whole family so that members talk and listen to each other, clarify each other's views and beliefs, explore differences and learn to communicate the variety of feelings they experience. The caregiver senses from the family their desire to continue the process within the relationship, their readiness to explore feelings and cope with their pain.

It is difficult to touch people in grief. The bereaved are lost in the depths of themselves and cannot always be summoned. When a child dies, the parent searches within for a reason, hoping to find some way to make the nightmare end. It is difficult work because we do not want to touch such sadness and pain and because the agony affects us and makes us ache and recoil to protect ourselves and our loved ones.

FOCUSING WITH THE FAMILY

The grieving process is complex. The numerous variables in this process include family interactions, sources of support, previous losses and grief patterns, cultural norms, and views of the future.

The process of grieving does not progress in predictable sequential order. Responses in grief are varied.

The responses of the family who have lost a child member are multiple, change with time and vary in intensity. Each member of the family is affected by the death, and each will deal with the loss differently. These differences may be the cause of distance and misunderstanding withing the family. The caregiver can help each member appreciate that the other is also grieving and recognize these differences in expression. We idealize harmonious relationships but because of our normal differences, dysynchronous patterns are more common. The communication gap widens and needs become exaggerated; disappointment and feelings of rejection become stronger. In working with the bereaved, it is important to recognize the variety of feelings and the differences in their expression, and especially the need to work on communicating. This approach will assist family members in deepening the bonds between them rather than widening the gaps.

Feelings may be put away to try to quiet the storm within only to find that it rages again in some crisis situation as, for example, a subsequent pregnancy. This is especially true when the realization that soon a child will be born and the possibility of this child dying comes closer and closer. It is not uncommon for siblings to feel directly responsible for the death of their brother or sister. Each member of the family wonders "why." Grandparents grieving the loss of their grandchild witness the death of part of their own child and grieve this loss also. They may wish that they could give their own lives in exchange for the child. They bargain, feeling that they have lived long enough. If the grandparents are the primary caretakers of the child, this adds yet another dimension to their loss.

Families are complex systems. They have their own patterns, boundaries and power. The family is more than (and apart from) the sum of the individuals who comprise it. We cannot lump individual expressions into a family expression of grief. Similarly we cannot assume that fathers and mothers feel the same after their child's death. Nor can we exclude brothers and sisters, regardless of their ages, from personal grief. The family may also include extended family members, friends and others who become natural support networks. All grieve for the dead child.

The family system changes when a child member dies. The survivors must put the system in order again, restructure it so that it continues to work for them. In a sense then, the energy for restructuring is part of the work of grieving; that is, it is energy needed to reorder life and integrate this loss into living and functioning. Since death creates a crisis in the system, inherent in this change are the possibilities for creative alternatives. If the family is using their energy to deal with the change and the intensity of meaning that it has for them as individuals and family members, this energy can be repatterned or rechanneled to promote health in the family system. The caregiver can serve as a catalyst for communication and direction within the system.

A child's death affects the whole family. Often one can observe a balancing of roles within the family. For example, the father may listen and support the mother in her need to talk about their child and her fear and guilt while she supports him by dealing with the many telephone calls from family and friends. In healthy relationships, roles tend to be reciprocal. When the child dies, it is useful if the scales can be tilted and balanced to allow each partner the necessary release. It would be helpful for a caregiver to act between family members, easing the pressure and providing them with a new view of each other. Their communications will increase and they will be better able to respect and appreciate their differences and provide each other with needed space. This can often be catalyzed by the presence of an objective person, while it would be impossible if they were alone because of their reliance on the pattern in their relationship. The caregiver becomes involved with the family primarily to encourage them to relate more meaningfully with each other, not to relate through another person.

Children in the household will be deeply affected by the death. The surviving child may feel guilt and a sense of responsibility for the death. One seven-year-old was able to say that she felt that it was her fault that the baby died. The evening her baby sister died she had stayed overnight at a friend's apartment This was her first time sleeping at a friend's home. Usually she shared a bedroom with her baby sister. Her conviction was that she could have saved her sibling had she been home.

Parents very often need a great deal of help in planning how to handle the other children's reactions and interpretations of death. It is helpful to use the word *dead*, to understand that young children may comprehend death as permanent, and that they frequently believe that they, too, will die. Above all they need to feel safe, secure and loved. Children often cling to their parents, thinking that if they are nearby, nothing will happen to them. Parents may find this very comforting but also very difficult when they feel emotionally depleted. Questions seem endless and the parents are tearful at the mention of the dead child's name. If parents want another child soon, they may find it helpful to recognize that this child will be different. They will feel joy for the new life and sadness for the loss of their dead child. In addition, they will be fearful that the new child may also die.

Another grief reaction of parents involves sexual expression. Sexual expression is a form of communication that is an important part of a relationship. Touching and pleasing each other may be difficult for parents when reminded that their child is dead. If the mother or father feels that another child is out of the question, sexual abstinence may result in an effort to eliminate the possibility of another pregnancy. It is not uncommon for couples to feel differently about a subsequent child. One partner may want another baby and the other may feel the only way that they can cope is to prevent this. The caregiver can assist the couple to recognize their differences and the reasons underlying these differences. Discussion of anatomy, physiology and birth control can be useful.

Often the emergent theme for the role of caregiver is the reinforcement of the individual's and family's strength and ability to select alternatives. Frequently, grieving parents are blind to the strengths and assets that they truly do possess. It is crucial not to minimize a parent's situation in any way, especially with phrases like "you are young" or "you can have another child." Avoiding euphemisms is crucial. Parents often feel that they have failed so profoundly as parents that their actions or omissions took their child's life. Identifying strengths helps in the healing process.

Individual and family coping behaviors vary also with cultural beliefs about what is acceptable and appropriate and how the period of grieving is managed. Grief for a child transcends all boundaries. Reactions and responses will differ from person to person, family to family and culture to culture. One cannot measure the degree of pain or the significance of the lost child by expressed behavior alone. Expressions of grief may be dictated by family rules and societal values of acceptable behavior and may be very different from the caregiver's beliefs and practices. Shock and disbelief are necessary defenses of the family against the reality of loss. This numbing effect will alter natural responses. What is felt in grief cannot be reduced to words.

The family in grief will contend with many experiences in the world outside, with others' perceptions and reactions. They may be feared or avoided. They may be blamed or expected to forget and put away their sorrow. They may be asked to fill themselves up again either with another child, a hobby, a new responsibility or a job. Because their pain is so great outsiders may feel drained and unable to be available for them. Or they may be held responsible for their child's death, for failing as parents. They may be accused of doing something wrong or of not caring enough. There is often no reason or rationale for this blame, but the parents are held responsible as others feel threatened by the child's death. While the caregiver may not be able to join with the bereaved parents in the experience of losing their child, that caregiver can be with the parent in the realization of powerlessness. That seems to be the place where all can join hands and minds and feelings.

True support is difficult to give because it means listening, accepting and encouraging the family. Support comes without question or questioning unless these are helpful to the family. Connections with available networks of support can be useful because the parents require ties with life. Otherwise they may feel no reason to live. Families without available support need to be connected to caring people and agencies by referral. Follow-up must also be ensured or else the bereaved will be put at risk.

WORKING WITH THE FAMILY OVER TIME

Encounters with the bereaved family may be short or long, immediate or years after the child's death. Regardless, the operating principles are relatively constant. The caregiver engages in the human experience of reaching out to another and communicating in a helpful and healing way by exploring issues, opening communication, and offering information that may assist the family in anticipating and dealing with their grief reactions and experience. The caregiver provides an atmosphere for expressing grief. Regardless of when the caregiver begins to work, the grieving family has felt, thought and heard a variety of reactions and responses to their child's death and has come to their own unique conclusions. Each family has a story to tell, a tragically painful story of all that preceded the death of their child and all that followed, of all that was said and not said. For many parents, explanations and interpretations ultimately lead back to them and foster a sense of self-blame for their child's death.

Immediate reactions to a child's death will vary from hysteria or rage to collapse and withdrawal. An environment that fosters and accepts all responses is helpful. Encouraging family members to come together at this time promotes communication among members. Questions, fears and fantasies surface and are dealt with, increasing understanding of each other's responses. This is a time to assist the family in accepting the reality of the death. It becomes a time to see and confirm that their child is dead. No mistakes were made. If desired, it is also a time to begin the painful process of separation by saying good-bye. Parents may choose to hold their child, dress their child, talk to him or look at him, and become aware of the presence of death. Families will require space and time and permission to grieve.

Usually families are confronted with a multitude of decisions at a time when decision making is most arduous. An autopsy may be requested, and parents' concerns and fears about the procedure will emerge. The child continues to be part of the parents, and they continue to provide care to their child, so the decision to submit their child to an autopsy is a painful one. Funeral and burial plans also have to be made. Even though planning may be difficult for the parents, they should be encouraged to make these decisions. Often plans are made by well-meaning relatives or friends to save the parents from this difficult task. Later, parents wish that they had exhibited more control and planned a service as a way of caring for their dead child and themselves in their grief.

The caregiver serves as a resource person knowledgeable about community advocates and agencies that may be useful to families. The caregiver may be helpful in locating a funeral director or local association of funeral directors who can assist the family with special needs. The family's choice can then be supported. It also helps to be familiar with the local death investigation process. In situations of sudden and unexpected death or death by homicide or suicide, the medical examiner or coroner's office typically will be involved. Families can be informed of protocol and provided with concrete information and direction so that procedures are anticipated. Knowledge about death certificates and public burial funds may be of immeasurable benefit to the family. Such information can be written down for families. Finally, local resources for information and counseling can be provided. Particularly helpful is the name of a parent contact from a helping organization that may also sponsor bereaved parent group meetings or telephone contact.

In working with the family members immediately following a child's death, it is essential to support expressions of grief. The body is in a state of numbness, and expressions of grief need to be released from within the bereaved person. The form that these expressions take is varied. Caregivers must deal with their own personal fears and responses to another's pain and hopefully be able to allow any expression as acceptable as well as offer anticipatory guidance about subsequent grief behaviors. It also helps the family members to realize from the start that each individual grieves differently and may not feel the same at the same time.

Although the bereaved parent may feel that life is senseless and has little meaning, these expressions need to be differentiated from suicidal thoughts. It is one thing to believe that it would not matter if one fell out a window or stepped in front of a car and another to plan one's own death deliberately. Although it is difficult to predict behavior, some clues of the parent at risk are outright sharing of the suicide plan, being alone without support and putting one's life in order as though separating one's connections. It is imperative that a bereaved parent not leave the hospital or emergency room alone, leaving the dead child behind and leaving without human contact and support. In addition, some defined contract can be made with the family members for follow-up and a telephone number provided for the parents to call should they want to reach out for information or support.

If the child died suddenly or at home, it is critical for the caregiver to speak with the person who found the dead child. Agonal signs, or signs that relate to death itself, may be misinterpreted as neglectful behavior. Under these circumstances, the parent may have no recourse but self blame. The caregiver can be very helpful in explaining the facts.

Also in this immediate period after the death of a child, it is helpful to assess the family's ability to sustain itself through the ensuing chaos. Usually someone will emerge as the natural leader and provide direction. Concrete and helpful information can be provided to this person. Lastly, one determines if support networks in the local community can be mobilized to assist the bereaved family.

Working with the family over time allows the caregiver to

- explore issues,
- open communication,
- offer information and provide anticipatory guidance.

The caregiver may then explore issues with the family such as the meaning of their child to them; the disruption in their lives; their understanding of the cause and circumstances of the child's death; their impression of what they were told about their child's death and what they really think happened, since discrepancies may exist; reactions from others including neighbors, police, ambulance and emergency room personnel; their immediate problems; and how they would like the caregiver to be of assistance to them. The caregiver can support the family in the exploration of critical issues by focusing on their strengths and fostering their abilities and decision-making capabilities. It is also important to gather together other extended family members and supportive people whom they identify as issues are raised and discussed.

To assist in opening communication within the family system, the caregiver must first look for blocks in communication within the family. Are family members blaming each other or protecting each other from their own feelings or from difficult tasks? One member may even be made a scapegoat or used as the focus for expressions of anger. The caregiver should be mindful of the shattered sense of self and self-esteem that the parents may be experiencing. If there are surviving children in the family, the parents should be encouraged to take responsibility for these children, thereby fostering the restoration of self-esteem. Specific concerns of siblings, which parents find most painful to deal with, are usually unresolved areas of pain for themselves. The caregiver can ask questions that are helpful to the whole family in opening communication.

Anticipatory information about the wide range of normal grief reactions is helpful since there are few guideposts to assist bereaved parents in comprehending their grief. Issues related to blame, self-blame, blaming spouse, God, doctors and so forth should be sought so that blame becomes recognizable, understood and focused. In order to bear grief, parents need in some way to ask why their child died, to know where to place blame. Information about grief reactions can be helpful in sorting out the facts from distortions.

The family will need guidance in planning what to expect tomorrow, the day after that and next year. For instance, future episodes of acute grief are part of the normal grieving process, especially at significant times like the child's birthday, the anniversary of his death, other days or places that were special to the family, and the birth of subsequent children. The family will also need assistance in helping them cope with extended family members and community reactions. Sometimes feelings can be normalized if they can be anticipated—like the pain and jealous rage experienced at the sight of another's healthy baby, alive and well and living with his parents. Powerful grief responses follow a child's death whether sudden and unexpected or known and anticipated. The finality of death is always a shock. Emptiness cannot be eased by anticipation.

Information about grief reactions is beneficial primarily as a way of preventing misinformation. Sometimes family members may gather more and more information as a way of defending them-

selves by intellectualizing their responses and distancing themselves from their feelings. Too much assistance runs the risk of
becoming less than beneficial and even rendering the parents
helpless and unable to gather the energy to mobilize their own
strengths and discover their own course of action. Working with
the bereaved family is best accomplished through clarification of
feelings and thoughts; promotion of congruent messages, feelings
and reactions that are in harmony; and validation of the significance of all expressions of grief. The family is viewed as a vital
system, not incapacitated and helpless, but capable and strong.
Grief has valleys, plateaus and peaks. Parents do not get steadily
better, but they move through a process, experiencing the depths
and heights of emotion. Pain does lessen with time, although it can
return in an instant. Sharing memories helps to soothe and heal
because memories continue to live in the survivors' minds.

The caregiver determines with the family when phases of the
grief work are completed. Grief needs time to be expressed and
dealt with; it cannot be forced. So many factors come together to
influence specific grief responses including past experience with
death, previous losses, how they have been dealt with, the person's
sense of inner peace and control. The need for solitude may be so
strong or the anger or powerlessness so pervasive that the caregiver
may be rejected or become the recipient of these reactions. The
bereaved parents may be agitated because others expect them to
return to normal living long before they are ready to pick up the
pieces and restore some semblance of order in their lives. Death
also precipitates other family problems, which demand attention
before the family is free to grieve their lost member. Poverty,
medical problems and problems with housing are only a few influ-
ences that confound the process of grief.

Sometimes the bereaved need permission from others to enjoy
themselves in spite of their sorrow. It is perfectly normal to want
to feel happiness and be released from anguish while still loving
and missing the dead child. The family lives with their dead child
as part of the family's identity. They also live beyond the child as
time brings change and newness.

The caregiver offers to the family continuing availability, re-
flecting the long-lasting nature of family bereavement. It is impor-

tant for a caregiver to remain available to the family. It may take months or years before a family can raise and deal with issues related to the child's death. For others, reaching out requires energy that is now dissipated. Continued outreach to the bereaved family is essential.

In working with bereaved families, the caregiver comes to realize that more is shared than is different. We all are survivors ultimately. Caregivers open themselves to the impact of death in their own lives, demystify death, and commit to providing care to survivors.

Books about Death and Grief for Children and Parents

Books for Young Children and Parents Dealing with Death Through Loss of an Animal

The following listing of children's books about death and grief is a special sampling. It contains books that introduce young children to the experience of death and to the myriad of feelings that children have in response to this important event in their lives. These references for the preschool and young school-age child present the theme of death gently and poignantly through the death of a beloved pet. The books are listed by age groups.

The Dead Bird by Margaret Wise Brown. Addison-Wesley, Reading, Massachusetts, 1958.

This simply told story is about a group of children who discover a bird, realize it is dead, and prepare to bury it. (3 to 5 years)

Lifetimes: The Beautiful Way to Explain Death to Children by Bryan Mellonie and Robert Ingpen. Bantam Books, New York, 1983.

With large illustrations, the book tells about beginnings, endings and living in between for plants, animals, and people. Dying is as much a part of living as being born. (3 to 6 years)

The Tenth Good Thing About Barney by Judith Viorst. Atheneum Publishers, New York, 1971.

This is a poignant narrative by a small boy of his feelings of sadness when his pet cat dies. The boy and his parents bury the pet and discuss the warm memories they have of Barney. (5 to 8 years)

Accident by Carol Carrick. Seabury Press, New York, 1976.

Christopher is helped by his father to express his grief when his dog Badger is killed by a truck. Together they search for a special rock to mark his grave. (6 to 8 years)

Currier and Ives. *The Burial of the Bird* (1872-74). Lithograph. Reproduced with permission from the collections of the Henry Ford Museum and Greenfield Village, Dearborn, Michigan (negative number B3636).

Badger's Parting Gifts by Susan Varley. Mulberry Books, New York, 1984.

All the woodland creatures love old Badger. When he dies, they are overwhelmed by their loss. Then, they begin to remember him. (6 to 8 years)

Books for Older Children and Young Adolescents on Death of a Sibling or Close Friend and Grief

These books for older children specifically consider a close friend or sibling's death and the family's response to this loss. Again, they are arranged according to age groups.

A Taste of Blackberries by Doris B. Smith. Thomas Y. Crowell Company, New York, 1973.

The author conveys the experience and feelings of an eight-year-old boy whose best friend Jamie dies accidentally. The boy and his family, along with Jamie's family, deal with the myriad of questions and feelings engendered by this unexpected event. (8 to 9 years)

Charlotte's Web by E.B. White. Harper and Row, New York, 1952.

The large, gray spider Charlotte dies after saving the life of Wilbur the pig, her close friend. (8 to 12 years)

Confessions of an Only Child by Norma Klein. Pantheon Books, New York, 1974.

When Antonia, who is nine years old, anticipates having a new sibling who will share her parents and home, she has mixed feelings. However, when that baby dies, she is very sad. (8 to 12 years)

The Magic Moth by Virginia Lee. Seabury Press, New York, 1972.

This is the poignant story of a family of seven whose middle child, 10-year-old Maryanne, dies at home from an irreparable cardiac defect. The parents handle the death and the responses of the surviving children sensitively. (10 to 12 years)

Little Women by Louise May Alcott. Macmillan, New York, 1962 (originally published 1869).

This favorite classic presents the story of Beth's invalidism and eventual death. Interwoven throughout are Beth's own sense of her dying and the responses of her family and friends. (10 to 14 years)

Beat the Turtle Drum by Constance C. Greene. The Viking Press, New York, 1976.

In this touching story, the effect of the sudden death of the 11-year-old child on her older sister and parents is told with warmth and sensitivity. (10 to 14 years)

Bridge to Terabithia by Katherine Paterson. Thomas Y. Crowell Company, New York, 1977.

This book portrays the grief of Jess, a 10-year-old boy in rural Virginia, who becomes close friends with a newcomer, Leslie. Leslie dies while trying to reach their hideaway, Terabithia, during a storm. (10 to 14 years)

Straight Talk about Death for Teenagers by Earl A. Grollman. Beacon Press, Boston, 1993.

With reassurance and compassion, Grollman explains normal reactions to the shock of death, the impact of grief on relationships, dealing with pain, funerals, and much more, including a place for readers to record their memories. (13 to 19 years)

Guidelines for Parents and Other Caregivers

Included for the parent is a brief listing of carefully selected books that offer guidelines for communicating with children about death. Also included are a few books that offer more detailed information about certain subjects.

Anna: A Daughter's Life by William Loizeaux. Arcade Publishing, New York, 1993.

An eloquent memoir of a father's loss of his baby daughter. The author shares his sorrow with heartbreaking honesty and power.

Death and Dying: A Bibliographical Survey by Samuel Southard. Greenwood Press, Westport, Connecticut, 1991.

A rich reference source compiling many annotated books and journal articles dealing with a wide range of topics related to death, dying and grief.

Explaining Death to Children by Earl A. Grollman. Beacon Press, Boston, 1967.

This is a simple and straightforward presentation of children's concerns and questions about death and adult answers and responses.

Death Be Not Proud: A Memoir by John Gunther. Harper and Row, New York, 1949.

This memoir, written by his father, is a loving tribute to his 14-year-old son John, who died of a brain tumor.

Hour of Gold, Hour of Lead: Diaries and Letters of Anne Morrow Lindbergh. Harcourt Brace Jovanovich, New York, 1973.

These diaries and letters contain a rich account of the early years of the Lindbergh marriage and of the pain and loss of their abducted child. Living without their child is chronicled poignantly.

How Do We Tell the Children? Helping Children Understand and Cope with Separation and Loss by Dan Schaefer and Christine Lyons. Newmarket Press, New York, 1993.

In a commonsense approach this resource uses straightforward, uncomplicated language to explain the facts of death to children and teens, and shows how to help children cope with their feelings of grief, fear and loss.

In the Midst of Winter: Selections from the Literature of Mourning, edited by Mary Jane Moffat. Vintage Books, New York, 1992.

From Catullus to Camus, from Shakespeare to Virginia Woolf, from Lady Ise to Adrienne Rich, great writers express the inexpressible. Arranged in sections that correspond to the stages of mourning, this collection is invaluable and utterly unique.

Sudden Infant Death Syndrome: Who Can Help and How, edited by Charles A. Corr, Helen Fuller, Carol Ann Barnickol and Donna M. Corr. Springer Publishing Company, New York, 1991.

Written by the leading authorities in the field, this compendium focuses on three issues relating to SIDS: families needing help, professional and lay caregivers who can provide help, and the various means for offering help.

Suicide: Prevention, Intervention, Postvention by Earl A. Grollman. Beacon Press, Boston, 1988.

An invaluable resource providing information on suicide statistics and giving advice on how to recognize the warning signs of a potential suicide attempt, how to intervene when a suicide has been attempted, and how to comfort families and friends who have lost a loved one to suicide.

Talking about Death: A Dialogue between Parent and Child by Earl A. Grollman. Beacon Press, Boston, 1990.

To be read with one's child, this book contains a story about the death of a grandfather, which can be adapted easily. The story is followed by a text directed at helping parents understand children's concepts of death at different ages.

The Anatomy of Bereavement by Beverley Raphael. Basic Books, New York, 1983.

Wise and compassionate, this comprehensive book on bereavement shows how people at all stages of life cope with grief, loss, and pain. Exploring human bonds and death, a special chapter is devoted to the death of a child.

The Cry of Rachel: An Anthology of Elegies on Children, edited by Sr. Mary Immaculate. Random House, New York, 1966.

In this brilliant piece of original scholarship, Sr. Mary Immaculate has assembled elegies on children that reflect the diversities of tradition and modes of expression and the universality of parental grief on the death of a child.

When Pregnancy Fails: Families Coping with Miscarriage, Ectopic Pregnancy, Stillbirth, and Infant Death by Susan Borg and Judith Lasker. Bantam Books, New York, 1989.

A compassionate sourcebook offering up-to-date information on pregnancy loss, its possible causes, coping and resources for support for grieving families.

The Cruelest Death: The Enigma of Adolescent Suicide by David Lester. The Charles Press, Publishers, Philadelphia, 1993.

An incisive overview of current knowledge about the growing phenomenon of adolescent suicide, providing information useful for prediction and prevention.

Questions and Answers About Suicide by David Lester. The Charles Press, Publishers, Philadelphia, 1989.

Provides clear answers to more than 100 of the most frequently asked questions about suicide, dispelling many myths and misconceptions.

Young People and Death, edited by John Morgan. The Charles Press, Publishers, Philadelphia, 1991.

This book gives practical advice and guidelines that parents, teachers and counselors can use in their daily activities with young people who are facing terminal illness or the death of siblings, friends and other loved ones.